PRAISE FOR

Unfiltered Marketing

"Denny and Leinberger capture the profound truths and deep realities of leading and marketing in a rapidly evolving world of digital platforms. The raw transparency we are experiencing through these platforms changes the game entirely. It's no longer a manipulative 'battle for your mind' as Trout and Ries once said. It's a battle for hearts and raw conscience."
—Blake Irving, former CEO of GoDaddy

"Denny and Leinberger have an unparalleled understanding of marketing and the value of raw experience—be it person to person or on Zoom. If you read this book, you will be wiser and more successful in reaching people with your brand."

—Joanna Coles, TV producer and
former chief content officer of Hearst Corporation

"This is a must-read for marketers as well as political campaign professionals. We can't look at candidates or political campaigns the same way anymore. Candidates can now speak to us directly and voters want a direct connection with the people they vote for, just like consumers do when seeking a connection with the products and services they purchase. *Unfiltered Marketing* gives us an unvarnished look at how smart campaigns and smart marketers need to work in 2020 and beyond. This read will make you better and smarter."

—Jim McLaughlin, campaign pollster and public opinion expert

"A must-read guide to making sense of our topsy-turvy world—a world in the midst of cultural, social, business, and tech changes (to name but a few). Useful in marketing, sales, operations, or . . . (frankly) . . . in navigating modern life."

—Ann Handley, chief content officer of MarketingProfs and *Wall Street Journal* bestselling author of *Everybody Writes*

"I'm in the business of cultural trends and have seen a lot of presentations and data on the topic. These insights are different. They resonate on a whole new level and are immediately actionable. Once I read this, I had an urgent need to rewrite the marketing plans I was about to present to clients. In a world where the consumer owns their own marketing journey, this book is a must-read."

—Anne Bologna, chief strategy officer of CrossMedia

"At Zeus Jones, we help businesses imagine, then create, a new world. Since we opened our doors, we have believed that brands are defined more by what they do than what they say. Steve and Paul understand this. They have uncovered research insights that build on that premise, adding valuable nuance and texture. And with people depending on their digital relationships more than ever through a global pandemic, their conclusions have become even more poignant. This is so much more than a marketing book—it is a window into today's cultural landscape and a playbook for how to thrive in that world."

—Rob White, cofounder of Zeus Jones and former president of Fallon Worldwide

"Trust has always been a valuable resource, and its value is especially high today because it is now so scarce. The barriers to entry into the ranks of the trusted are high and likely to remain so. But *Unfiltered Marketing* shows the way forward. It is a unique source of guidance for breaking down barriers and regaining trust. Full of insightful, actionable advice."

—Ralph Whitehead, professor of journalism (retired) at the University of Massachusetts at Amherst

UNFILTERED
MARKETING*

*Messaging That's Raw, Unscripted & Real

5 Rules to Win Back Trust, Credibility, and Customers
in a Digitally Distracted World

Stephen Denny and Paul Leinberger

Foreword by **Brian Solis**, author of *Lifescale*

CAREER
PRESS

This edition first published in 2020 by Career Press, an imprint of
Red Wheel/Weiser, LLC

With offices at:
65 Parker Street, Suite 7
Newburyport, MA 01950
www.careerpress.com
www.redwheelweiser.com

ISBN: 978-1-63265-178-5
Library of Congress Cataloging-in-Publication Data available upon request.

Interior by Timm Bryson, em em design, LLC
Typeset in Adobe Garamond Pro

Printed in Canada
MAR
10 9   8 7 6 5 4 3 2 1

*To Nicholas, Alexander, and Christine—in hopes that
the goal is always clear, no matter how difficult the path.*
—Stephen Denny, 12/9/19

*To Susan and Harper, for their constant support,
good-humored patience, and love.*
—Paul Leinberger, 12/9/19

CONTENTS

Part 4 THE FUTURE

FOREWORD: MAY I HAVE YOUR ~~ATTENTION~~ INTENTION PLEASE?

Long gone are the days of brand style guides, messaging by committee, jargon, and communications and sales techniques.

Stephen Denny and Paul Leinberger are about to take you on a journey to win your trust. But before they can do that, they have to earn your attention. And before they can do that, you have to believe that by giving them your time and focus, they will help you learn something so valuable, something you don't already know or believe you need to learn, or that they offer something more compelling than you can figure out for yourself.

The only chance that they have to succeed in winning your trust is to be raw, unscripted, and real with you.

If you think about it, the same is true for the people you're trying to engage in your work. If you're reading this book, you probably have something to say or sell or teach. You're hoping to reach a desired audience and help them understand that by connecting with you, they'll be better for it. But ask yourself, why should anyone trust you? Why should anyone give you their attention or give you the gift of earning their trust?

If you take one more step down the rabbit hole, you'll see that your audience is also hoping to reach their audiences.

And so it continues . . .

Everyone has something to say, but very few believe they have something to hear. We live in a world where audiences have an audience of audiences. But what happens if no one is listening and everyone is talking? What happens when no one is learning and everyone is teaching? The answer is, nothing helpful or productive.

Somewhere along the way, we've all come to believe we're entitled to an audience. The democratization of information, media, and connections introduced unprecedented power. But with that power should come great responsibility. Instead, we became enamored by access, reach, and reactions. We exchanged attention for distraction. We collected responses and followers like they were coins spilling out of a slot machine. We traded openness, compassion, and empathy for the illusion of popularity and influence. We became convinced that our audience was there to support our views and beliefs, lift us up, support us in times of need, and validate how we see ourselves and how we want others to see us. All of this became not only our new normal, but our life support system.

We weren't ready.

All of this change came at considerable costs. Truth. Trust. Values. Leadership. Attention is now intentionally exploited. Facts are now debated with beliefs. Truth is now possessive—with truth lying in the eye of the beholder. Leadership is now dictated by misdirection, misinformation, and gaslighting. We live in a time, for better or for worse, when everyone knows everything. Everyone has access to the most accurate sources of information. Everyone is safeguarded by their truth. Tribes are formed around belief systems.

So, what do we have to learn? What do you have to learn? Everything.

There are two ways to change behavior—you can intentionally manipulate it or you can inspire it. We see what the world looks like with relentless command and control all around us every day. To inspire it, takes honesty, and that honesty has to start from within.

To earn someone's trust starts with intention, an intention to find common ground. That means you have to be willing to change and you have to know enough about someone else to learn how to add value.

For them to listen, for someone to let down their guard, to open a personal door to attention and ultimately connection, also requires a common language. To find common language, you have to discover alignment in personal values and aspirations. You have to identify and speak to their inner fire. You have to connect with who they are today and who and where they could be tomorrow. And, there has to be total alignment and agreement that together, directionally and fundamentally, you're better and stronger than before.

To break the cycle, you have to shock the system with radical transparency and radical empathy.

This is a time to be real.

This is a time to be open.

This is a time to see and feel what you couldn't before.

This is a time for raw, unfiltered engagement.

Denny and Leinberger will take you on a journey of personal and professional transformation to help you help those who matter most. You'll learn how to rehumanize engagement with an audience of audiences. The result is the cultivation of a more meaningful and productive community where trust, truth, and the value of connection thrive once again.

Now, may I have your ~~attention~~ intention please? Let's turn the page and begin.

—Brian Solis
digital anthropologist, optimist,
human being and author of *Lifescale*
@BrianSolis
BrianSolis.com

The Impact of Technology on Culture

So I'm told by a reputable person they have killed Osama bin Laden. Hot damn.

—Keith Urbahn, the former chief of staff to
US Secretary of Defense Donald Rumsfeld,
via Twitter at 7:24 p.m. EST, May 1, 2011,
two hours before President Barack Obama
made the announcement on national television

On the first of May 2011, at 12:58 p.m. local time, in Abbottabad, Pakistan—roughly 4:00 p.m. EST in the United States—Sohaib Athar took to Twitter to complain about the noise outside his apartment, unwittingly becoming the man to break the news that US Navy SEALS were on their way to kill Osama bin Laden.

The Pakistani IT consultant was working late in his home office when he heard helicopters overhead. It turns out he was living 250 meters away from the place where bin Laden had been hiding for the past three or four years.

Five and a half hours later, the White House issued an all-media press release—at 9:30 p.m. EST—saying that the president would make an important televised address in one hour. Obama eventually made it to the podium at 11:35 p.m. to confirm that bin Laden had been found and killed. By that time, of course, anyone with a smartphone and a Twitter handle had already read the news, from experts and from complete random strangers, and celebrations had already begun in earnest.

Keith Urbahn, the former chief of staff to US Secretary of Defense Donald Rumsfeld, was the first semiofficial source to suggest that the reason for the presidential address was the death of bin Laden, tweeting, "So I'm told by a reputable person they have killed Osama bin Laden. Hot damn." He hit Send on this tweet at 7:24 p.m. EST. Twitter peaked at roughly 7,000 tweets per second during the intervening four-hour time frame, culminating in two singular events: the highest-viewed presidential address of the Obama administration as well as the official death of the mainstream media as the place one goes for breaking news.

It would be easy to point to this moment as being the moment the concept of "raw" was born, and, in all honesty, this wouldn't necessarily be a bad seminal moment to officially declare the beginning of what has become an increasingly mainstream movement. Mr. Athar's tweet was the stone hitting the surface of a global pond that literally went around the world 7,000 times a second, finally reaching each of us, one way or another, on our phones—well before the unconnected among us found out what had happened the old-fashioned way.

THE TRIUMPH OF THE
PERSONAL OVER THE PUBLIC

We can look to other events and the people who brought us closer to the moment, beyond the bin Laden killing. Mention the Arab Spring and the name that comes immediately to mind is former NPR correspondent Andy Carvin, who, at his most fevered pitch, was posting and reposting up to 1,000 tweets a day in the early moments of 2011. The eighteen days of protests, centered in Cairo's Tahrir Square, ultimately claimed an official death toll of 846 people and toppled the regime of President Hosni Mubarak. But for anyone looking for the raw feed, the only place to go was Carvin's Twitter feed. The irony is that he never set foot in the Middle East during the entire Arab Spring. He merely transmitted what was coming to him via Twitter from thousands of people on the ground and in the Square itself as the protests were happening. Anyone entering Carvin's feed with questions was immediately answered by those on the ground, not just providing background and context but often with live video, hand-held and first-person, from protesters in Cairo in the Square, all within minutes of posing the question. It was a sobering, raw experience. A casual Twitter user sitting on the couch in the US could have a woman in Cairo sending smartphone video of the shots fired and the tear gas happening at that exact moment. Somehow, waiting for the news at night was no longer important. We knew more than the anchors on television did.

Likewise, when the Red Shirt protests erupted in Bangkok in March 2010, people turned to Michael Yon, who reported on the insurrection from the five-star Dusit Thani hotel, literally overlooking the barricades and on whose front steps Yon reported that after a career of war theater operating (as both a soldier and reporter), he was first shot (it was a ricochet—he was unharmed, unlike a colleague several meters away who lost his life). Another surreal experience, we can only imagine: ordering room service and enjoying the amenities of a true Thai luxury hotel in the heart of Bangkok's financial district and having an RPG (rocket-propelled grenade) hit and explode three floors above. Yon's reporting was full feature-article length, available to read on his blog, but absolutely on the scene and in as close to real time as possible.

These events are important for our discussion because, for the first time, we truly had access to the same raw information that the media had, and we often had it first, depending on our intellectual curiosity and the quality of our questions. The technology in our pockets is as powerful as a live television network, both for receiving the messages coming in from Cairo or Bangkok as well as for transmitting it out, Carvin-like, to our respective audiences. But this discussion is hardly confined to news media. This disintermediation and direct access to raw information—and raw experience—have been mainstays in entertainment for years.

THE IMPACT OF TECHNOLOGY ON ENTERTAINMENT

We can look back to 1989, the year that *Cops* first' aired on television—a show dedicated to capturing a day in the life of police officers doing the most routine parts of their jobs with shaky hand-held cameras, trying to keep up while an officer pursues a suspect through a Florida back lot in the dead of night. While not captured in real time, *Cops* gave us first-person video—capturing the immediacy and raw imagery of police action as few had ever seen it before. Fast-forward to the present, and we can see how livestreaming has revolutionized this simple idea with *Live PD*, A&E Networks' hit show, a mash-up of *Cops* and *Monday Night Football* that gives viewers multiple video streams coming in from police departments across the country, essentially live and in real time, with a studio panel of experts providing context for what viewers are actually seeing. We'll hear from A&E's Rob Sharenow later in this book about what *Live PD* has meant to the culture and to the network. This is a trend in entertainment that will only grow, as other networks take steps in this direction as well.

We see this trend having a powerful footing in the music business, where festivals and live music events have become the hottest segment of the industry, outpacing streaming and album sales in growth and share. Musicians are searching for ways to close the gap with fans, creating unique business models for concert venues that include special access, while others search out ways to create novel technological listening experiences, often entirely virtual and having more similarities to massive online gaming than the traditional definition of a sit-down concert.

We see this trend expanding in sports as well. Take NFL football, for example. In 2009, we saw the tipping point of old analog televisions giving way to HDTVs in the United States, thus moving from the 4:3 aspect ratio to the now ubiquitous 16:9 wider screen. This change brought more than just sharper pictures. It changed how production crews captured football, allowing for more players to be shown on the field at the snap. This is as close to the all-knowing eye-in-the-sky "all 22" view that coaches use to break down their opposing team's offenses and defenses, and it has ushered in a new era of game-day analysis. We can now see almost everything that's going on, right from our couches, just because we upgraded our television sets back in 2009.

Fast-forward to the present, and we see the beginnings of "raw experience" in sports front and center in the NBA, with teams and the league itself taking this shift very seriously. NBA Commissioner Adam Silver is quoted as saying, "If you're sitting courtside, you hear the referees talking to the players . . . you hear the players talking to each other . . . you can often hear the coach talking to the players . . . how can we bring that richer experience directly to our fans?"[1] The LA Clippers basketball team has an answer to that, in part, having launched its Court Vision smartphone app that shows real-time data on players, likely court movement based on their offensive sets, and an overall sense of context while the game is being played.

We see this trend having a tremendous impact in politics, where old notions of detached candidates giving stump speeches and appearing in carefully controlled television interviews have given way to politicians live on social media: tweeting, streaming, producing raw videos, and breaking down every barrier possible between the issues, the personalities, and the voters. The old rules are out the window. The former social media director of Donald Trump's campaign, Justin McConney, recalls the moment he realized that the genie had leapt out of the bottle, saying, "The moment I found out Trump could tweet himself was comparable to the moment in 'Jurassic Park' when Dr Grant realized that velociraptors could open doors . . . I was like, 'Oh, no.'"[2] Oh, no, indeed. Personal technology has broken down what few barriers existed between candidates, politicians, and the vulgate, allowing for some of the most larger-than-life characters in history to literally say (and livestream) anything that comes into their heads, day or night, for better or worse.

We even see this trend in the porn industry, so they tell us, with the advent of livestreaming, virtual reality, 360-degree camera views, and interactive devices all coming together to deliver a greater sense of authenticity and connection to what has been historically more aptly described as a one-sided experience.

From news to entertainment to sports to politics to porn, this shift to "raw" has defined the leading edge of the cultural experience. Old notions of gatekeepers and safe distance have given way to disintermediation, direct access, and raw experience.

BUSINESS IS DOWNSTREAM FROM CULTURE

Now we're seeing this emergent trend appear in the business world more frequently, and its emergence is long overdue. This is what we're going to spend the bulk of this book discussing.

In an age of collapsing trust—when Wikileaks, scandal, and fake news from both the public and private sectors dominate our news feeds and where we now have access to the same sources of information that the traditional gatekeepers have historically kept to themselves—the only thing we now trust is "us": our own eyes, our own senses, and our own judgment.

We don't want pundits or PR handlers telling us what to believe.

We want the unfiltered truth in as raw a manner as possible.

We want the raw feed, the leaked emails, and the live video stream. We want the CEO on camera, on the spot, telling us what's happening—now, not in a month after hoping we've forgotten about the IT outage or the product failure. We want direct access, complete visibility, and a look at the data itself—without a spokesperson or media talking head getting in the way telling us what we're supposed to believe.

The faster we understand and adopt this emerging trend, the sooner we can make our mark in the world. Ignore it, and even the most beautiful idea will get lost in the digital whiteout of modern culture.

OUR GOAL

This book will set out to explain how this idea can positively impact your venture—be it growing your company, launching your campaign, or simply persuading an increasingly jaded audience to your point of view.

We've set the scene well, at this point, and hopefully have been clear in defining the playing field. Our goal going forward is to lay out a series of sequential steps, with each building on the previous work, so that you can fully understand not just the "what" but the "why" and the "how" behind this emergent trend and the framework behind it.

Our structure is simple.

We will start this discussion by delving into the unfiltered foundation of raw—what created this set of expectations and desires—illustrating the idea with stories, interviews, data, and analysis. In each chapter, we will spend considerable time and effort illustrating the key takeaways that have the biggest implications for businesspeople looking to apply these lessons to their companies. As both authors and principals of Denny Leinberger Strategy come from senior management roles and have deep experience consulting with consequential clients, we live in this world and believe the biggest value we can add to this body of work is to ensure that readers not only grasp the big picture behind the ideas but also have ample ammunition for using these lessons in their daily lives at work.

Our first chapter is "Seeking Control in an Out-of-Control World," a primary global macro trend that underpins everything we will discuss. This chapter will describe the collapse of trust in the institutions around us and our resulting drive to regain some sense of control over our lives. This loss of trust and our desire to overcome it form the foundation upon which raw has emerged.

It is important to understand the difference between our desire to wrest control back from the forces working to deprive us of our data, our individual privacy, and our ability to influence our outcomes and the more simple idea of "the collapse of trust," which others have reported on in years past. That we're living in an age defined by this collapse of trust is a given and a position we have no interest in debating. We believe this to be true because our global research has unarguably suggested this to be correct. However, there's more at play here, and ending the analysis prematurely leaves a tremendous amount of insight—and action—on the table. Explaining to a business leader that consumers and strategic partners lack trust in the institutions around them doesn't lead anyone to a next course of action. Pushing ahead and pointing out that everyone around us, all around the world, is striving to regain some sense of control over their lives are of paramount importance. Articulating this point— along with relevant examples and data points—spurs the student of business to action. That's our goal, so the distinction is important to lay out up front.

Our next three chapters discuss raw in a disaggregated way, breaking the idea into different component pieces to ensure that you, the reader, can see the full nuance and complexity of this idea, animating it as thoroughly as we can. Our goal, as always, is to give you models upon which you can temporarily try on solutions and either use or discard them based on your unique circumstances. This adaptive persona method of problem solving is deeply rooted in storytelling and gives us the opportunity to apply lessons from elsewhere to our often-insular industries. Our three animations of raw will be explained in detail in chapters 2 through 4.

Because we are "seeking control in an out-of-control world," and because we have shifted to raw in its many forms, we now have a new challenge we must address: limp, middle-of-the-road messaging is no longer audible to a market bombarded with messages, raw or not. We must be willing to be bold, to break through, and to occasionally be uncomfortable with how far we push ourselves. We must align with the values of our customers—but not cross the very thick line that separates authentic values from moralizing on issues on which we have no authority. We, as consumers, are willing to follow brands that have true values. But if you overstep your bounds and start telling us what to think about issues that aren't ownable or easily defined as in your area of expertise, we'll turn on you. And woe to the brand that takes an edgy position and then retreats in shame at the first sign of pushback. We're willing to listen to bold brands, but we can't stand cowards. This is our discussion of "heroic credibility" in chapter 5.

In chapters 6 and 7, we shift gears and synthesize learnings from what we've explored in the preceding chapters. First, in chapter 6, we will look at how technology has impacted culture and essentially flipped the polarity of the brand/consumer relationship. To consider our brands as being either business to consumer (B2C) or business to business (B2B) is increasingly naïve, particularly when viewed against a landscape where technology plays such a profound role in cultural change. We are now living in a C2B world—a consumer-to-business world—where the individual, not the brand, is in control of the brand experience. When we consider this shift— where individuals armed with smartphones can now capture and rebroadcast their thoughts to their extended networks about our performance, comparison shop while in the very act of shopping to compare prices and availability from not just alternative retailers but also from the very brands themselves, and where every possible distraction imaginable can and does come between the brand and the transaction—it should change how every marketer approaches the job. Once we embrace this idea, the shift to C2B goes a long way in rehumanizing the digital relationship.

A second outcome of this framework impacts how we tell stories in this digitally distracted marketing landscape. In an age of raw, is storytelling dead? In our opinion, no. This hunger for direct, disintermediated access to the data and the newsmakers plays a central role in persuading a distracted, jaded audience to not just hear your words but lower their mental spam filters and give you their full attention. But it doesn't have to be the only role. We'll explore the impact and purpose of longer-form storytelling and its symbiotic cousin, raw, in chapter 7.

One of the great discoveries in developing this body of work over the past several years is the power of combining these key ideas into a holistic system. When we look at the implications of combining "seeking control in an out-of-control world" plus "raw" plus "heroic credibility," we see a system of thinking that suggests bold actions across many areas of interest in the enterprise.

In chapter 8, we'll look at how this framework impacts leadership and creates a blueprint for those seeking to understand how to best navigate these difficult times, where each employee is hyperconnected with peers both inside the company and out, where some of whom might actually be brands in and of themselves.

Viewing this framework through the lens of brand loyalty, we'll explore the likely future of brand loyalty, where shared values and bold messaging dictate reach and preference, and the willingness to stand up for yourself despite the inevitable backlash from the social media wolfpack can multiply your winnings. This is the conversation in chapter 9.

Understanding the implications on culture will be the topic of chapter 10, particularly with a view toward management and collaboration in an age of increasingly virtual, decentralized workforces. How we communicate, manage, and persuade colleagues, peers, and direct reports who no longer sit down the hall is of paramount importance in this new age of remote collaboration.

We will wrap up this discussion in chapter 11 with three likely scenarios we see potentially unfolding in the intermediate future, drawing on everything we've seen thus far.

As one Fortune 500 marketing chief told us, "This forces us to rethink how we do . . . everything."

We hope you find the same inspiration from this work.

We strongly believe there are a finite number of truly big ideas in the world at any given time, and we think this is one of them.

The unfiltered, raw approach is going mainstream.

PART 1

The Rules

The five rules that we're presenting in the following chapters are based on our multiyear Culture & Technology Intersection study, which we first launched in 2016. We set out to explore the impact of technology on culture as it relates to the brands we buy, the digital footprints we manage, and the work we do in an increasingly distributed workplace. Our consulting work with clients, ranging from Fortune 500s to global multinationals to highly motivated, "Giant Killer" mid-caps, has helped us hone this message and accelerate what many have come to see as a revolutionary way of seeing their respective businesses.

These are not statements or observations about the likely future.

These are actionable insights, big concepts that if carefully implemented can change the trajectory of your business, your campaign, or even the evolution of your personal brand.

Read them as such. Apply them as you are able.

Let's start with the first big macro trend—one that underpins everything that is to follow: seeking control in an out-of-control world.

CHAPTER 1

Rule #1: Seeking Control in an Out-of-Control World

But out of the gobbledygook, comes a very clear thing . . . you can't trust the government . . . you can't believe what they say . . . and you can't rely on their judgment . . . and the—the implicit infallibility of presidents, which has been an accepted thing in America, is badly hurt by this . . .

—H. R. Haldeman, chief of staff,
Monday, June 14, 1971, 3:09 p.m.,
quoted from audio recordings taken during
a meeting with President Richard Nixon in the
Oval Office on the release of the Pentagon Papers

THE SEEDS OF DISILLUSIONMENT— PENTAGON PAPERS, 1971

We always prefer to view history through our own personal and recent experience, but before the Panama Papers, before Wikileaks and Julian Assange, and before Edward Snowden, there was Daniel Ellsberg and the Pentagon Papers.

Looking back to the early 1970s from a technology perspective is virtually impossible for many, but it's critically important to understand not only the cultural impact of this foundational event but also the long odds it overcame to make it into the public eye. We assume that leaks and exposure of carefully hidden lies and other misdeeds are a function of cell phone cameras, flash drives, and Tor uploads. This event makes Ellsberg and the Pentagon Papers so instructive because the lack of access to what most of us in the twenty-first century would even recognize as technology makes the contrast with modern examples all the more striking.

There have been ample books, movies, and articles published that outline the story, with varying degrees of drama. Daniel Ellsberg's resumé following his receiving a PhD in economics from Harvard shows tenures at the Pentagon, the State Department, and later at RAND Corporation, where he contributed to a top-secret study on the conduct of the Vietnam War. While compiling the RAND study, however, Ellsberg became aware of evidence that the Lyndon Johnson administration had used falsified information to bolster its case for expanding American military involvement in the Vietnam War. Ellsberg's conscience wouldn't let him ignore what he was seeing. His decision to make copies of the top-secret report and other related documents and send them to the press and select members of Congress began a domino effect that culminated in a Supreme Court case giving the publishers the green light to print the documents in their entirety. Ellsberg was shortly thereafter found innocent of all charges after it surfaced that government agents with a direct reporting relationship to those close to the White House had engaged in a series of dirty tricks, including burglarizing Mr. Ellsberg's psychiatrist's office to look for embarrassing material and attempting to poison him with LSD at a public event to incapacitate him.

How do we gauge the impact of the Pentagon Papers? Their publication didn't stop the Vietnam War, which continued for another four years. Absent the newly released movies and other pop culture references to this event, most contemporary readers under the age of fifty would never have known what they were or why they were important.

The cultural impact of the Pentagon Papers must include that it contributed to the sentiment of unrest that embodied the 1960s and early 1970s, particularly as it related to the eventual downfall of the Nixon administration. But perhaps more importantly, the publication of the documents accomplished two critical goals. First, they educated the American people, for the first time, that we the people couldn't trust the government, couldn't trust their judgment, and could no longer view the office of the presidency as something infallible—which from a cultural perspective was a clear departure from the past. Second, given the subsequent Supreme Court ruling allowing the press to go to print with the top-secret documents, they shifted the balance of power from those holding the secrets—the government—to those exposing those secrets to the public.

It's this second impact that concerns us most in this discussion: a US Supreme Court decision ruling allowed anyone in a journalistic position to publish highly sensitive information, even to the point of being classified as top secret, in the service of the public interest. For those in the US, the impact of this decision clearly emboldens "leakers of conscience" and sets the precedent that those exposing wrong-doing—from either public or private sector sources—are to be supported and believed.

The Pentagon Papers ultimately brought down the Nixon presidency, mostly due to the president's and his inner circle's reaction to their publication. The threatened impeachment and ultimate resignation of a sitting president was an earth-shaking cultural moment for the United States. And trust in the institution has never fully recovered.

EXPOSURE IN THE AGE OF INSTANT ACCESS

Fast-forward to the present, and we see so many examples of high-profile leaks—in terms of importance, volume, and frequency—that the Pentagon Papers, were they to break today, might feel like a marginally newsworthy story. Julian Assange and Wikileaks, Edward

Snowden, and others are ever-present in the news cycle—and accessible via your mobile phone directly through their presence on Facebook. Chelsea Manning, Reality Winner, and others are now household names. Recent studies show that public trust in government is below 50 percent in the United States, with trust in the media at an all-time low. Perhaps with full correlation and causality, we also see that leaked information is globally viewed as more trustworthy than official company press statements by an almost 2:1 margin.[1]

But viewing the collapse of trust purely through the lens of diplomacy or foreign policy misses the bigger picture as it relates to modern life.

We see countless examples of companies large and small skirting the edge of propriety regarding what they are collecting and archiving, what they are doing with our information, and what they are promoting or suppressing.

Amazon's home smart device, the Echo speaker powered by Alexa, was prominently featured in a high-profile Arkansas murder case in 2017, which hinged on Amazon divulging audio recordings that may or may not have been captured after the device was activated by its "wake" word. While Amazon assures us that the device doesn't capture ambient audio, the internet is filled with examples of accidental recordings (if you own an Echo, you've no doubt had this happen to you) as well as theoretical and actual examples of hacking the device to manipulate when it's activated.

Similarly, Google acknowledged in October 2017 that its Home Mini smart device was in fact listening and recording all ambient audio in some users' homes twenty-four hours a day, seven days a week after a blogger from *Android Police* broke the story.[2] It has since been reported (by Google) that the glitch has been fixed and applied only to a limited number of early release beta products sent to reviewers.

Samsung famously warned users in 2015 that all spoken words, including "personal or other sensitive information," in the presence of its smart televisions were being recorded and sent to third parties through its voice recognition capabilities. Worse, Samsung advised users that even if they opted out of its SmartTV voice recognition feature, ambient audio would still be captured.[3]

We can view any of these examples as cases where we should give the brand the benefit of the doubt. All have nondisclosure policies, all have security procedures in place to safeguard private information, and all are using unattributable data to improve their services.

And yet.

And yet it's easy to see how each of these examples, not to mention countless others, can be interpreted as individual bits of evidence that when all viewed together prove that these companies and other entities do not have our best interests at heart and are perfectly happy to capture our everyday conversations for the purposes of commercial exploitation or worse.

KEEPING UP IN AN AGE OF TECHNOLOGICAL ACCELERATION

Events and advances are simply moving too fast for us to keep up. Watching a Silicon Valley technology executive getting grilled by Congress is akin to watching a pith-helmeted explorer trying to explain the magic that is a flashlight to a group of elder paleolithic tribesmen. There is so little common understanding between them that a conversation—let alone an informed interrogation, replete with sensible follow-up questions—is virtually impossible. The goal of ethically or legislatively constraining technology seems unattainable, and as a result the trust gap grows wider.

The fundamental question—and problem—of our times has thus become: how do we make sense of the tensions between technology and culture and trust?

"There were a number of serious panics—serious issues—in the 2016 election," Murtaza Hussain of *The Intercept* told the author in an interview on January 10, 2018. "Fraudulent news being published, hacking and distributing information that blurred the lines between activism and journalism or even state-sponsored activity. Technology has advanced to the point where people could do things like this. So our legal norms, our cultural norms, our legislation can't keep up with what's technologically possible. When we look at what's coming down the line, this crisis will escalate. I see no evidence that our norms are catching up. I think technology is starting to lap us. It's exceeding our ability to even keep up with what's going on."

And yet when we look at the collapse of trust in the broader picture, from government to big business to technology companies and others, there is a hunger on our collective parts to be consumers of leaked information and violated privacy, regardless of our personal views on the ethics or legislative oversight we might or might not be able to develop to constrain it. In this case, the ubiquity of mobile technology plus a lack of trust plus the collapse of privacy equaled Wikileaks.

"The Iraq War in 2003 and the financial crisis in 2008 were two very serious blows to people's trust in their institutions—and journalists really failed in their jobs to shape information to put it in intelligible form for the public," Hussain explains. "And there was a real hunger on the part of people who became disillusioned for the 'real story' without spin. Wikileaks seemed to satisfy that desire. There was a lot of good will towards them. Wikileaks is possible because of advances in information technology, but such an institution would never have come about if there weren't failures in our institutions that created a demand in the public for disintermediated information."

How do we draw a draft conclusion at this point? We lack trust in the institutions around us, we realize that technology is moving faster than our ability to constrain it, but we're fascinated by all the truth we now have access to in this post-apocalyptic privacy landscape. So, we're OK with it. Are we?

THE LOVE/HATE RELATIONSHIP BETWEEN PRIVACY AND TRUST

It's important to draw a thick line separating the ideas of "privacy" and "trust." The same technology platforms that capture and disseminate hacked information in the lofty name of the public good are the ones that leak our own information into the hands of anyone willing to buy it wholesale. We trust these technology platforms; this point is unarguable, no matter what we say, in the sense that we willingly share every possible detail of our lives on them with the understanding that they're a means to an end. They're convenient ways of communicating and sharing our lives with our close network of friends, but when questioned, we readily acknowledge that these platforms are more than likely using these shared insights, photos, and comments in ways we don't necessarily like. In this instance, the fondness of sharing plus the instant endorphin rush of validation times the zero value of our concern for personal privacy (and our unwillingness to say no, despite the terms and conditions we checked off when we signed up) equaled Facebook.

"We've signed over everything to these companies," Hussain continues. "We're almost unable at this point to not adopt what they put out, they're so radically powerful at shaping our society. We sort of took what they were offering willingly; we trusted them not fully understanding the philosophy behind what these programs and platforms really embodied. [Mark] Zuckerberg has been open about how Facebook will wipe out privacy around the world. They've warped the culture in such a way that it's hard to have this conversation."

Beyond the obvious use cases of sharing on social media, how do we view the technology that's closest to us—in our homes?

WHAT DOES THE DATA TELL US?

In our most recent study, 60 percent of US respondents expressed concern that smart devices in their homes may be listening to them and collecting information without their knowledge (close to half of

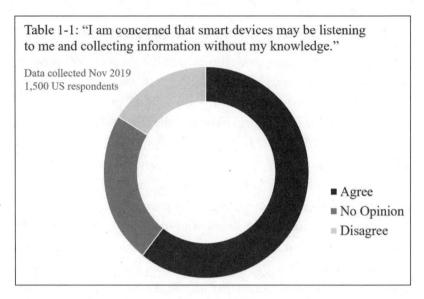

Table 1-1: "I am concerned that smart devices may be listening to me and collecting information without my knowledge."

Data collected Nov 2019
1,500 US respondents

- Agree
- No Opinion
- Disagree

those remaining expressed no opinion). In previous studies where we've collected global insights, we've seen similar attitudes in China, Germany, and the UK, with only Japan having expressed more trust in the security (and intentions) of their devices.

Beyond the narrow question of smart devices capturing the ambient audio in our homes and using it for nefarious purposes, we are increasingly skeptical of how technology companies are safeguarding our data. When asked, US respondents overwhelmingly agreed that brands routinely fail to take their privacy seriously, with 76 percent agreeing with the statement. In other words, this is not a question of a data point taken in isolation, but of a major consumer sentiment wave.

As a culture, we've become increasingly distrustful of technology—not just companies that provide technology and the occasionally cavalier attitude many have shown toward the security of their users' data, but also the security of the platforms themselves and their vulnerabilities to hackers.

We're also concerned about how safe our sensitive personal information is when stored in the cloud. Two-thirds of Americans

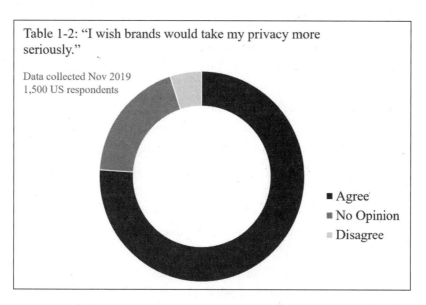

Table 1-2: "I wish brands would take my privacy more seriously."

Data collected Nov 2019
1,500 US respondents

- Agree
- No Opinion
- Disagree

are worried that their important personal information stored in the cloud—from financial and health-care data to photographs and personal data—will be stolen or used against them. Worse, a full 84 percent of Americans don't want their sensitive personal information stored in the cloud to reside on servers in countries they don't trust. So much for life in the post-Snowden landscape.

Beyond active data collection and storage, however, Americans are also concerned about passively collected data, from biometrics to location, with more than half concerned that data collected from their wearable devices—fitness trackers, mobile phones—is likewise vulnerable to hacking or misuse. Interestingly, the other countries surveyed all report similar scores on these three points. All are genuinely concerned about cloud security and particularly worried about which countries host the servers on which our own personal sensitive data resides, with slightly lower scores on wearables.

The Internet of Things (IoT) provides another example of cautious optimism balanced by concern over security. More than half of Americans would be willing to pay more for an IoT-enabled connected device only if there was confidence that it was secure from hackers, with a further quarter of respondents registering no clear opinion. This number compares to roughly two-thirds of Chinese respondents, just under half for Germany and the UK, and roughly a third of Japanese respondents.

Perhaps one of the most striking examples of measuring trust—trust in institutions or in data and technology platform integrity—is determining how many people have covered up the webcam on their laptop. We all remember the now famous photograph of Facebook's Zuckerberg announcing the acquisition of Instagram; it inadvertently showed that he was using an encrypted browser and had covered up his webcam with tape. Lest we think that such actions are the sole domain of the Citizenfour crowd of Snowden conspiracy theorists and self-described privacy aficionados, understand that a full 42 percent of US respondents have taken the step to obscure their laptop cameras. This act is fascinating because it's not an attitude but an action taken in response to a perceived security weakness and a fear of the consequences. When we've polled global respondents in previous studies, their results have mirrored what we've seen in the US. Nearly half of all citizens in much of the civilized world don't trust the security of their most personal devices.

These sentiments, from concerns over data security and privacy, speak to a mainstreaming of what was once thought to be a subsegment of hypersensitive conspiracy theorists. We care about where and how our data is stored, we wish the companies we entrust our data with were as concerned as we are, and we're taking safeguards to protect ourselves wherever we can.

SEEKING CONTROL IN AN OUT-OF-CONTROL WORLD

Given this collapse of trust and the increasing concern we have over how our private information is managed by the companies with whom we've entrusted it, we find ourselves increasingly exposed, both intellectually and emotionally. We no longer trust the institutions around us that we've traditionally grown up assuming are trustworthy. We no longer trust that the companies charged with safeguarding our personal and private information are taking their roles as seriously as we would wish. We are, in short, sensing that we are no longer in control of our own destinies, that the system is rigged against us, and that no one really has our best interests at heart any longer.

Against this backdrop of abandonment, it's clear that we're seeking ways to regain a sense of control over a world that is increasingly spinning too fast for us to keep up. Just look at how our attitudes have changed regarding how we define personal success. Traditionally, we defined success as the accumulation of material things—the trappings of success. For decades, Americans and others have responded that success, to them, was owning a large home in a prestigious neighborhood, driving a luxury car, and having financial wealth and other similar material accomplishments. Until recently, this has certainly been the case. But then the script flipped.

In our efforts to seek control over our lives, Americans now say the top signs of success are focused on regaining control. The top response, at 67 percent, was "being physically fit and in good health," followed by "having control over my time" at 64 percent, "living within my means" at 62 percent, "living a highly self-sufficient lifestyle" at 50 percent, and "working for myself" at 39 percent—the last of which was two percentage points above the first materialistic choice, "having a lot of money," which came in at 37 percent. It's interesting to note that of these choices, "having control over my time" was chosen as a sign of success by a margin of 3 to 1 over owing an expensive car or premium brands back in 2016, when we first ran the study. In our most recent survey in 2019, prior to this writing, this delta grew to an almost 5 to 1 margin. This attribute had almost three times the number of responses that owning a large house received.

To be clear, it's not that these "control" attributes simply outscored the "materialistic" choices that makes this point worth discussing;

it's that these "control" attributes were significantly higher than the highest "materialistic" choices available. If we look back at consumer sentiment data over the past several decades, this hasn't been the case. Success has always been a function of "what I have"; today, success is defined by "how much control I have over my life and my outcomes."

Indeed, when we simply ask whether we'd like to lead a highly self-sufficient lifestyle, depending only on ourselves, we see half of Americans in agreement, with a slightly higher number of women than men in agreement.

These responses signal a huge shift in values, for the United States and for the world, and importantly they need to be viewed against this larger backdrop of the collapse of trust.

It's important as we view major shifts in consumer sentiment, from the collapse of trust to our increasing desire for control over our lives, to also take into consideration another major cultural shift, namely the democratization of technology.

THE DEMOCRATIZATION OF TECHNOLOGY

Often, when you hear the expression "democratization of technology" used, it is immediately conflated with the "consumerization of technology," which speaks to a much narrower trend of the blurring of home versus professional-use products. When we speak of the democratization of technology, we acknowledge that today, access to technology has enabled each of us to create, capture, collaborate, publish, comment, and editorialize, all with tools we have easy access to at any time—often in our pockets.

Think of how far the democratization of technology has progressed since the publication of the Pentagon Papers. In 1969, Daniel Ellsberg began copying the documents that were eventually to be published via traditional media—the *New York Times* and the *Washington Post*—in 1971. The collection of documents ran some 7,000 typed pages. He created, with colleague Anthony Russo, close to two dozen copies totaling well over 100,000 typewritten pages of copy, all made on late 1960s-era Xerox machines—then, still quite rare and exotic pieces of office equipment. (Imagine if he'd had to rely on carbon paper, a commodity most readers won't have any knowledge of.) The time needed to create this entire body of work is mind-boggling, particularly when we realize that he was at risk of exposure the entire time, and exposure, as we were to learn, came with a potential maximum federal prison sentence of 115 years had he been convicted.

If the Pentagon Papers were to be published today, how would things be different? They would have been copied onto a flash drive, assuming the leaker were able to defeat safeguards against such measures, or a hard drive would have been removed from the premises. Perhaps the documents would simply have been uploaded via an encrypted email account to a secure browser or pushed onto the web via self-publishing tools and promoted via social media and similar online entities. What took two years of incredibly dangerous work could have been condensed to seconds.

We don't need an exhaustive analysis of the explosion of technological resources available to the average citizen in the developed world to understand the full extent of the democratization of technology, but a few salient points help put things in perspective.

Data from the Pew Research Center shows that smartphone penetration, internet access, and social media usage among adults have reached well beyond mainstream adoption, suggesting that the average citizen now has access to instant information as well as the ability to share it wherever they are.

- Smartphone penetration in the US is 81 percent as of 2019.[4]
- Internet access in the US is 90 percent.[5]
- Facebook usage among adults is 69 percent in the US, with YouTube usage at 73 percent.[6]

Smartphone users globally not only have access to the internet but also are able to view more information in richer formats more easily. Mobile download speeds now average 20.28Mbps, with many Western European countries in the 40–60Mbps range and the US at 26.32Mbps.[7]

Each of the preceding data points suggests an increase in access to information for the average citizen, both from traditional publications as well as from peers. Taken as a whole, however, the picture is more complex. We are now living in an age of instant access to information from all sources, available wherever we are—at home, on the street—with a growing capability to capture information and securely upload it or share it to an ever-widening group of connections, who in turn can share it with their connections in a viral expansion.

All of this points to a culture of visibility, where keeping secrets is harder than ever. Snowden, Manning, and others like them are now armed with the digital tools that allow the moral equivalent of millions of Pentagon Papers–sized document dumps to be moved in seconds. Capturing hidden video is instantaneous. Time and volume are now removed as constraints.

With the democratization of technology, everyone is now not just a citizen journalist but also an editor and publisher capable of broadcasting to a global audience from the convenience of their own mobile phone. We'd be remiss if we painted this as a rosy picture, of course; it's seductive and likely naïve to hope that all such uses of newly democratized technology are in the public good. One man's "citizen journalist" can be another man's "spy," after all. Regardless of the motivations, the information capture net is now spread wide. It's no longer just a case of war plans, government surveillance programs, or campaign emails. Bad behavior, once discovered, can be globally broadcast in minutes.

As a result, it's difficult for us to view big players in major institutions with anything other than skepticism. Our heroes have proven to be quite fallible. No wonder our cultural icons are falling like flies. Viewing all of this, it's clear why trust has collapsed.

What does this mean? Where do we go from here? By and large, humans are not nihilistic beings. We look for solutions to help us make sense of the world, even when the world seems to be spinning out of control. When we can't trust the institutions we've grown up with, the gatekeepers of information who have been traditionally charged with giving us the "news," or even the companies we've given our most private information to for safeguarding, whom do we trust?

THE FUTURE OF TRUST AND CREDIBILITY AND THE REEMERGENCE OF JUDGMENT

In an environment defined by fully democratized access to technology, where it's increasingly difficult if not impossible for a company, a candidate, or an organization of any type to keep poor behavior hidden for long, and when we no longer trust either the institutions or the intermediaries usually responsible for translating the firehose of information coming over the wire into digestible news, there's only one real and credible viewpoint that we can trust.

Our own.

We trust our own eyes and ears. And because we now *have* the evidence that the gatekeepers once kept from us, we are in a position to make up our own minds without the need for intermediaries to tell us what we need to think.

This is a unique turning point. The combination of the collapse of trust combined with greater access to the technology platforms that allow us to get access to the raw evidence itself and, in many cases, to create it, all points to a shift in what constitutes credibility in an info-immersive age.

We are in the early stages of a shift toward raw.

How do we define this new and emergent concept? Raw means we want to see the evidence ourselves—the raw video, the document dump, the livestream—so we can trust our own instincts and judgment and make up our own minds when we're asked to believe something by a brand or a media spokesperson. We want to come to our own conclusions. This trend is far more persuasive than all the apology tours and press releases could possibly be. Expect more of this as we go forward.

It's also important as we step off into a deeper exploration of raw to understand the wider implications of this emerging trend. This isn't simply transparency, a word so misused in recent times as to become virtually meaningless. Transparency has been used as a smokescreen by government and corporate interests for years to convey a sense of there being nothing to hide, while whistleblowers have pulled the curtains away from behind them. The concept of raw branches off into new avenues that allow the public to judge the truth for themselves—and, in certain circumstances, to become part of the process.

Understanding the concept of raw, as just described, is our starting point. But to fully comprehend the implications of how raw can positively impact your venture—be it growing your company, launching your campaign, or simply persuading an increasingly jaded audience to your point of view—requires that we focus on three major themes within the overall idea.

RAW MEANS UNSCRIPTED

We are looking for raw evidence in a form that is as unfiltered, unadulterated, and unvarnished as possible. We want the truth, shown to us as if we were there with you, seeing it first person, not a high production-value performance.

When the crisis hits, we'd prefer to see the CEO on camera, without the well-produced script and backdrop, explaining what has happened in as genuine and personal a manner as possible. We don't all need to be dynamic, arm-waving heroes, by any means, but we do have to be leaders who project the trust they hope to engender in their audiences. This kind of response beats a week's worth of silence followed by a slickly produced scripted video any day.

When we're trying to convince our audience that reality in the field is different from perceptions back in the ivory tower, a shaky hand-held video showing what's happening is more persuasive than carefully worded reports and all the PowerPoint in the world.

With a raw, unscripted approach, we no longer fear that our factories in Bangladesh will be exposed as sweat shops to an angry, activist-driven press. Direct access and visibility to manufacturing and supply chains are not only possible but increasingly a competitive advantage as brands look to promote their support of local businesses, wherever they may be. We like this sort of authenticity and respond to it when we can see it with our own eyes.

"Unscripted" delivers the first-person experience to a remote audience so they can project their own experiences, filters, and points of view to what you've shown them, allowing them to use their own judgment to form an opinion.

RAW MEANS IN-PROCESS

In-process means we're insiders, contributing to the development of the finished product, or at least closely connected to it throughout the process. We trust what we're a part of. We're more comfortable with outcomes when we feel we've been listened to. Living in an age of info-immersion gives us the luxury of not being surprised. We no longer want to wait for the evening news or for an official press release to come out. We want to know about it when it happens and want updates in real time.

In-process means we gravitate to opportunities where we can cocreate with brands and have access to frequent communication regarding events as they unfold. The information flow in a technologically immersive world isn't just one way. We now live in a time and place where dialogue is not only possible but expected.

RAW MEANS IN-CONTEXT

Context is a question of teaching as opposed to telling. Again, once we take the collapse of trust and the resulting desire to regain control of our lives as a given, our focus as marketers needs to address rebuilding credibility and trust. Providing the history and deep visibility into a product's origins, teaching how to interpret what the customer is seeing, and being a partner in exploration all rise to the fore. To many, *marketing* is a bad word now. We need to work around this constraint in a smart and lasting way if we are to regain trust.

When we have unparalleled access to digital content and live in a world where there is no expectation of privacy, our definitions of confidentiality or proprietary processes need to be reexamined. What we, as stewards of brands, believe is "top secret" usually fails to even elicit an eyebrow raise from our competitors, influencers, and potential customers. Sure, some things are secret. Let's acknowledge that this treasure trove of confidential trade secrets is far smaller than we think it is. The world is moving fast. What is utterly unique today is mainstream tomorrow—and likely comically obsolete next month. Understand, therefore, that educating your customers with the "how" behind what you do will likely rebound to your credit far beyond any feared loss of top secret-ness. The future isn't about being the hero with all the answers; it's about providing the context behind what your audience is seeing and teaching them how to interpret complex information so that they, too, become experts.

EXPLORING RAW IN DEPTH

The following chapters will provide deeper context and a greater understanding of the concept of raw.

We'll explore examples and case studies that illustrate best practices from as many walks of life as possible, providing an organic and qualitative understanding of how real-life people and brands have made this idea come to life for their audiences.

We'll share some of the data we've collected on the subject to provide a quantitative backbone to the qualitative, ethnographic stories.

And, as we've been living with all this data for a few years, having written and consulted on the implementation of these ideas, we'll add our own interpretations to see if we can help readers peer through the fog of uncertainty as we look forward.

We've come a long way since Nixon-era Xerox machines—in every sense.

CHAPTER 2

Rule #2: Raw Means Unscripted

There was an event where it started to come together. [During the Q&A at Consumer Electronics Show in 2013] the audience wanted to know what was on my mind [and] it hit a chord. From then on, I started to be the brand.[1]

John Legere, CEO of T-Mobile

The decision to become the "un-carrier" was not a marketing ploy. Something happened that was very personal and transformative, something that went far beyond any notions of "customer centricity" or "speaking the language of the customer." In an effort to simply be clear in a distracted and shiny-object obsessed world, T-Mobile CEO John Legere spontaneously snapped, as he describes above, and did something his buttoned-up competitors and even his legal department would never condone.

He went off-script.

He said things from his heart, in the heat of the moment, that not only served as a catalyst for his brand and business but also crystalized his own thinking regarding his role in the world and how his and T-Mobile's future would unfold.

This first illustration of raw is critically important in understanding persuasion and trust in a jaded world. When John Legere went off-script, he was not just speaking from the heart, in the heat of the moment; he was also demonstrating one of four human qualities that we desperately seek, but rarely find, in business leaders today. He was being candid and honest. He was being real.

To be unscripted tells the world that you are honest, trustworthy, authentic, and vulnerable.

"THIS WEIRD DISCONNECT"

Malcolm Gladwell, the author of *The Tipping Point* (2000) and *Talking to Strangers* (2019), told a *New York Times* reporter: "On every level, I feel like there is this weird disconnect between the way the world is presented to us in the media and the way it really is."[2] There is a disjuncture between what we are being told and what we either know or suspect to be the truth. It makes us wary, and understandably so. When you adopt an unscripted approach to leadership, the disconnect no longer exists.

Let's examine how we can go about making this happen. We are drawn to business leaders who are unscripted because this tells us that they are not afraid of making mistakes and they are willing to live with their own imperfections. Being unscripted implies a lack of deception. When we spontaneously speak, we run the risk of saying true things that perhaps we should have kept hidden from the public. Ask yourself why every lawyer and PR flack just off-screen when the CEO is being interviewed literally mouths the words they've planted with their boss and cringe whenever their leader, in the full glare of the spotlight, deviates from the script. What if our boss says the wrong thing and tells the media and the world what we are so committed to keeping secret?

This is the point. We, the public, want the truth. The honesty that comes from an unscripted moment is something that we value greatly, particularly in a world where we're used to being lied to. We want to hear the imperfections because they're what we relate to most.

UNSCRIPTED IS AUTHENTIC

To be unscripted means to be authentic.

In common parlance, authenticity is about "knowing who you are" and "getting in touch with your 'true self.'" It is one of those concepts that is difficult to explain and even more difficult to become. You can't tell someone to "be authentic" any more than you can tell them to "be spontaneous!" Yet how many times have you been given the advice (when applying for a job or before giving a big speech): "Just be yourself"? To be sure, that's good advice, if we only knew how to do that. Sometimes the gap between saying and doing can be very great indeed.

Oprah Winfrey attributes her success to her authenticity, and it is central to the way she lives her life. She explains authenticity this way: "Eventually, life reveals itself and shows you a mirror to help you see your own truth. Your real job on earth is to become more of who you really are. To live . . . what is pure, what is honest, what is natural, what feels like the real you."[3]

Oprah makes no distinction between her personal life and her business career; she lives by the same values and tenets in everything she does. However, it is fair to ask: is the concept of authenticity the same in the workplace as it is in one's personal life? Should you behave at work the same way you would in your personal life?

Take the concept of transparency and its relationship to authenticity. Transparency is sometimes important in a work setting, but it can also get you into trouble. Herminia Ibarra, organizational behavior professor at London Business School, tells a cautionary tale of a health-care executive who got a major promotion and decided that the best way to gain the confidence of her new staff was to be open and transparent. Cynthia, the executive, told her new staff: "I want to do this job but it's scary and I need your help."[4] However, her candor backfired, and her credibility was called into question. Years later, when Cynthia looked back on that experience, she told

Professor Ibarra: "Being authentic doesn't mean that you can be held up to the light and people can see right through you."[5]

To be sure, transparency is a virtue, but it is not a synonym for authenticity, and as Professor Ibarra relates, there is a time and place for transparency (in the workplace). Cynthia would have been better served to heed the advice of Anna Wintour, editor-in-chief of *Vogue*: "People respond well to those that are sure of what they want. What people hate most is indecision. Be decisive and trust your instincts."[6]

In a business context, authenticity is better understood as self-awareness, a willingness to take responsibility for one's own actions and for being honest with oneself. Authenticity means knowing one's strengths as well as one's weaknesses.

To others, to employees and the general public, it means "What you see is what you get." Others can trust you because you are consistent in your words, deeds, and ambitions. "You say what you mean and mean what you say." Others may or may not like what they hear, but they can trust that you are not going to say one thing to them and something completely different to someone else. They can trust that they are seeing the real you and not some phony image you want to portray to the world. That is what it means to be authentic in an unscripted sense.

We are drawn to people who are unscripted because they come across as genuine. They put us at ease because we don't have to wonder if they are telling us the truth. "Candor and honesty are rare in life," says psychotherapist Dr. Orna Guralnik. "People do better with the truth than without it."[7]

There is no better example of living an unscripted life than the late Steve Jobs. Jobs was much loved by his staff, but he was also feared. He didn't suffer fools, and he always said what was on his mind. As his brilliant biographer Walter Isaacson relates, "Jobs could drive those around him to fury and despair. He made a point of being brutally honest. That made him charismatic and inspiring, yet also, to use a technical term, an asshole at times."[8]

Jobs used to say, "This is who I am, and you can't expect me to be someone I'm not."[9] In his now famous commencement speech at Stanford University, he said: "Don't let the noise of others' opinions drown out your own inner voice. And most important, have the courage to follow your heart and intuition. They somehow already know what you truly want to become."[10] Jobs didn't have to say "you're brain-dead" as often as he did, but sometimes it was exactly what was needed to move things forward.

Jobs would probably have been a better leader had he been able to temper his darker impulses. However, the fact that his colleagues knew who he was meant he could be trusted and counted on. In his own eyes and in theirs, he was being both honest and real. And in part because of that, he created one of the world's most valuable companies. Jobs was authentic—and a wonderful example of raw unscripted.

Likewise, Anna Wintour, editor-in-chief of *Vogue* and artistic director of Condé Nast, whom *Forbes* has called "the most powerful woman in media and entertainment," lives an unscripted life. She works and lives by the motto: "Own who you are." And she goes even further: "Own who you are without apology."[11] Like Jobs, Wintour believes that it is important to be decisive and to trust your instincts. "You are leading, you are not following and that is a very important lesson to always keep in mind."[12]

There is a danger here that one could come away from the examples of Steve Jobs and Anna Wintour believing that authenticity is about always speaking one's mind and expressing one's opinions, damn the consequences. That would be the wrong conclusion.

Author Mike Robbins uses a concept he calls the "the authenticity continuum" to explain why always expressing one's opinions is not the same as "being authentic." "On one side of the continuum is phony." Those are the times when you tell white lies or pretend to be someone you're not. As you move down the continuum, you get to honesty. Sometimes if you express your honest opinion, you will find yourself in trouble. So you learn it is better to either alter your response or say nothing. However, explains Robbins, there is something on the other side of honesty. "Authenticity is on the *other side* of honesty. [It's] a willingness to let other people know who we really are and how we really feel."[13] It takes courage, he says, but when you do it, amazing things can happen.

UNSCRIPTED IS A WILLINGNESS TO BE VULNERABLE

As we said earlier, to be unscripted implies a willingness to be vulnerable. And vulnerability, as it turns out, is a valuable quality for another reason. To learn, you have to be open to other ideas, other ways of thinking, knowing, and seeing; you have to be vulnerable. It is at the heart of innovation, and here again, Steve Jobs understood this. He understood that to be innovative, you have to create a culture of learning. You have to be willing to take risks and make mistakes . . . and, most importantly, to learn from those mistakes.

Jobs once told one of this book's authors, Paul Leinberger, that innovation at Apple was an iterative learning process, not a magic formula that could be diagrammed and taught. It was a matter of trying something, realizing it wasn't quite right, and trying again. This would happen again and again until everyone was satisfied. He recalled that the original Macintosh was very much like that—try and learn, try and learn. Under Jobs's leadership, Apple was always taking risks, making mistakes, and learning from those mistakes. That is what has always set the company apart: that attention to detail, that drive to keep trying until it was perfect—sometimes even magical (as Jobs said at the launch of the iPad).

Alibaba, China's e-commerce giant, is headed by Daniel Zhang, who became Alibaba Group chairman and CEO in September 2019 when he succeeded Alibaba's visionary founder, Jack Ma. Much like Jobs at Apple, Zhang believes that learning—and learning from failure—is the lifeblood of the company. He told McKinsey & Co.'s Daniel Zipser, "We give our people a lot of space to try new things. It means you have to accept mistakes. The vast majority of innovations will result in failure; you have to acknowledge that. But the key is, can we learn from our failures?"[14]

UNSCRIPTED CONNECTS US

When you live an unscripted life, others are attracted to you because they sense your willingness to listen and your interest in connecting in a genuine or real sort of way. They are drawn to you because they know that you are willing to risk making mistakes and you are willing to live with your own imperfections. Your comfort with who you are suggests to others that there is a real possibility of developing a meaningful relationship, a real connection. Being unscripted opens you up to the world, and it invites others to follow your lead. Being unscripted helps build rapport and trust.

The most powerful aspect of living an unscripted life is that it is contagious. Others want to follow your lead. Because you are comfortable in your own skin and willing to take chances, you value learning far more than you value always being right. Your authenticity shines through and others are attracted to you. In our view, living an unscripted life is one of the defining characteristics of a twenty-first century leader.

UNSCRIPTED IN A CULTURE IMMERSED IN TECHNOLOGY

When we view this concept of being unscripted against the backdrop of a culture immersed in technology, we understand why it is so valued. The ability to manipulate what's been said through digital editing means the vast majority of what we're shown has likely been antiseptically scrubbed of any meaning before we see it. If the default setting is "propaganda," we become jaded to what we're being fed. In the never-ending avalanche of information cascading across our screens, it has become increasingly difficult to know what is true and what is false, what is worth paying attention to, and what is just noise. How do we know what to believe and who to believe?

In an age of citizen journalists, each armed with camera phones and broadcast media courtesy of their smartphones, it's not only hard for a company official to keep the truth under wraps, but it's also very easy for those willing to simply strip away the spin to be unscripted, in the moment, and refreshingly honest about problems, solutions, and leadership.

As such, we see forward-thinking executives using video—live or not—to communicate in a more human, less ignorable manner. Unscripted is perceived as more credible, less staged, and ultimately more persuasive. This approach encompasses everything from executive communications and traditional press release–type messaging to behind-the-scenes glimpses into how brands make what they make, to day-in-the life exposure to brands, brand use cases, celebrity endorsements, and more.

"The reason I know they won't be able to take advantage of what I do is that there's no f---ing way they're going to be able to spend their day doing what I do," John Legere, CEO of T-Mobile said.[15]

In an interview at the GeekWire Summit in 2014, Legere describes first joining Twitter while having dinner with his daughter and having T-Mobile corporate security call moments after his first tweet, fearful that the account was run by an imposter. From there, he describes the pressure he received from regulators and lawyers fearful of what might happen if the slightly larger-than-life CEO were to actually go full frontal off-script in front of the public. The rest, thankfully, is history. Legere lives off-script, interacting dozens of times a day with users, both present and future, on Twitter, where he's accumulated over 6.5 million followers—more than double what his entire set of competitors have, collectively. As his preceding quote suggests, he represents the antithesis of corporate-speak, as we can agree that there's no f---ing way legal would approve such a script.

And yet despite Legere's maverick personality and management style, T-Mobile's market cap has doubled under his leadership, and subscriber growth outpaces the competitors he loves to goad online. He understands the power of leading an unscripted life.

LIVESTREAMING: THE TECHNOLOGICAL EQUIVALENT OF UNSCRIPTED

Forward-thinking executives and brands are using video to communicate in a more human and relatable manner. One of the most popular ways of using video is livestreaming, and it is growing by leaps and bounds. Facebook, for example, introduced Facebook Live in 2016, and by 2018, one out of five videos on Facebook was a live broadcast. Overall, not just in terms of business communications, streaming video accounts for over two-thirds of all internet traffic, and it is expected to jump to (at least) 82 percent by 2022 according to Cisco.[16] And it is easy to understand why. According to this report, "80 per cent of people report that they prefer watching a live video to reading a blog, and 82 per cent prefer live video to social posts." That is why the number of marketers using video in their marketing jumped a dramatic 24 percent between 2017 and 2019, according to Hubspot.[17]

Livestreaming is, in many ways, the technological equivalent of unscripted. By its very nature, it is immediate, candid, personal, and authentic. The potential for making mistakes, of saying something that is not quite right, of drifting off the corporate line is always there. And that, of course, is its attraction. It comes across to viewers and participants as real—because it is. As Kathryn Minshew, co-founder of The Muse, has said: "Live video is a phenomenal medium for engagement because of the rawness, immediacy and authenticity of it."[18] "What streaming video does best is to allow brands to drop the corporate veil, connect human-to-human, and allow users to participate in brand storytelling in ways that enrich the customer experience," says Kathy Klotz in her Convince&Convert podcast.[19]

One of the most promising applications of livestreaming for companies is conducting live question-and-answer sessions. Experian, the global consumer credit reporting company, is using Facebook Live and Twitter in weekly livestreaming sessions to chat with consumers about credit, debt, student loans, and ways to manage and improve credit scores. The weekly sessions began as an experiment—to see whether or not there was an interest on the part of customers to talk live with Experian executives. The sessions quickly became popular, and, as of the middle of 2019, they had done well over one hundred chats on everything from "Tips for Home Buying" to "All About Love & Money." Using #CreditChat on Twitter, Experian has found livestreaming to be a "wonderful way to connect directly to consumers," and its credit chats have "reached hundreds of millions of accounts," according to Rod Griffin, director of public relations at Experian.[20]

Experian understands that the needs of consumers are changing, and the way they use technology needs to change with them. "We have seen some dramatic changes in the way customers want to consume information," says Barry Libenson, global chief information officer at Experian. "They are on a digital journey themselves and gone are the days when we could prescribe how they consume things. They want (information) in real time."[21] By engaging and responding to customers in real time, Experian has put a human face on the company and successfully changed the way its customers view it. Experian is no longer viewed as a cold, faceless, data-crunching monolith, but rather as an innovative firm dedicated to meeting the individual financial credit needs of customers worldwide.

Events and product launches are another opportunity for livestreaming, particularly for those that are high profile. On July 18, 2019, in one of the world's largest wooden structures that was once the home to World War II Navy dirigibles, General Motors did something it had never done with its storied sports car, the Chevrolet Corvette—launching the "Next Generation" Corvette via livestream. The dramatic reveal of the revolutionary mid-engine Corvette was livestreamed to the world and linked to all of Chevrolet's social media channels. The stream included Corvette video footage, a hosted preshow, and the reveal presentation.

Why livestream the launch? Barry Engle, executive vice president and president, The Americas, General Motors, explained: "With all the excitement, we don't want people to have to wait to experience it in person. We want them to start imagining themselves in their very own personalized mid-engine Corvette."[22]

This livestream was the most dramatic event in Corvette's history. According to General Motors, 471,000 tuned into the livestream reveal. It triggered massive online traffic to GM's websites, and the Chevrolet.com site recorded 2.4 million visits between July 18 and the end of July—a new record. By July 29, just ten days after the launch reveal, the first year's production was spoken for. "I think the orders have already hit the first year of production numbers," said Michael Simcoe, General Motors vice president of Global Design. "It is nearly sold out."[23]

Most automakers do not hold livestreaming launches for their autos and trucks, so it is difficult to compare Corvette's success with other livestreaming launches. However, it is fair to say, that in the future, when a company wants to draw attention to a new product it is launching, it will choose livestreaming. Technology companies like Apple and Microsoft have been livestreaming product launches for years, but this approach has yet to go mainstream in most businesses. That is about to change.

Another smart application of livestreaming occurs when brands take advantage of the interactive nature of the medium and publish interactive shows that highlight their products and solutions. Experian's Credit Chat is an excellent example of one type of series. It comes on at a set time each week, and just like a broadcast television series, people get in the habit of tuning in every week. Livestreaming shows are no different, except that you don't just watch; you have the opportunity to interact with the shows' presenters.

One of the first businesses to adopt a livestreaming format was CNN's *Anderson Cooper Full Circle*, launched in 2018. The show is similar in format to *Anderson Cooper 360°*, Cooper's nightly show on CNN. However, *Full Circle* is only ten minutes long, and it is highly interactive. Cooper takes questions from his audience, invites viewers to challenge his guests, and asks his audience to suggest topics for upcoming shows. The fast-paced show is very informal, with Cooper walking around the CNN broadcast center in shirtsleeves, and because of its interactive nature, viewers are more engaged. The program has a dynamism, intimacy, and a sense of connectedness that are a far cry from formulaic broadcast news shows. It is model that business executives could, and should, emulate.

Another fascinating example of the interactive nature of livestreamed programming comes from the world of cooking. The format of television cooking shows has changed very little since Julia Child introduced American TV audiences to the world of French cuisine in 1963. Livestreamed cooking classes are changing that. Instead of watching presenters cook a meal, viewers who tune in to a livestreaming cooking class can cook at the same time as the chef, getting pro tips and asking questions on-the-fly.

HelloFresh was one of the pioneers of the meal-kit delivery service business, and it was one of the first meal-kit services to offer livestreaming cooking classes. The brand wanted to make sure its customers got the same results at home as the online service promised. To do that, the brand created a live interactive cooking show where HelloFresh customers cook at the same time as the host. Streaming live, customers can ask the host questions, receive step-by-step guidance, and have a little fun along the way. This approach has proven a major success and helped the brand build customer loyalty in very competitive space.

One of the most ambitious interactive cooking shows was launched by the Food Network in late October 2019. It is a paid subscription service that offers live, interactive cooking classes with some of the world's top celebrity chefs, such as Giada De Laurentiis, Bobby Flay, and Rachel Ray. The streaming-video app, called *Food Network Kitchen*, lets users cook the same meal being prepared by the chef and ask questions during the class. "There is something special about taking a class live," said Peter Faricy, the head of direct-to-consumer at the Food Network's parent company, Discovery, Inc. "You can ask questions during the class. Someone may ask Bobby Flay: 'How much salt do we need in this?' It's about as authentic an experience as you can get."[24] You are cooking with a celebrity chef, and that chef is answering your questions as the meal prep progresses. How cool is that?!

To engage users even more, the Food Network has partnered with Amazon Fresh and other retailers to deliver all of the ingredients needed to make the meal. And beyond that, *Food Network Kitchen* has partnered with retailers including Amazon to sell the cooking utensils used in the classes. *Food Network Kitchen* broadcasts twenty-five live classes a week, has over 800 on-demand classes on its website, and includes over 80,000 recipes.

Companies and brands are using livestreaming in other ways as well. Livestreaming is being used to cover live events, like the Consumer Electronics Show, and important company events and announcements—for company town hall meetings, for conference panel discussions, and for behind-the-scenes looks at a company's operations. Livestreaming will continue to grow in popularity, because it is the technological equivalent of unscripted and an excellent execution of raw.

WHY LIVESTREAMING IS GOOD FOR BUSINESS

We live in a changed world. Customers are accustomed to high-quality video experiences in everything they do. Video increasingly dominates all forms of our communications, and consumers have come to expect high-quality video experiences from the companies they do business with. "Live video is becoming a necessity for companies. It's the best way to get your point across to as many people as possible," says Michael Weinstein, video studio lead at Deloitte Global.[25] Further, says Chapin Clark, executive vice president and

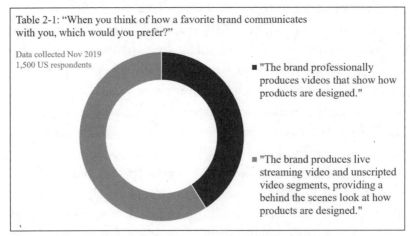

Table 2-1: "When you think of how a favorite brand communicates with you, which would you prefer?"

Data collected Nov 2019
1,500 US respondents

■ "The brand professionally produces videos that show how products are designed."

■ "The brand produces live streaming video and unscripted video segments, providing a behind the scenes look at how products are designed."

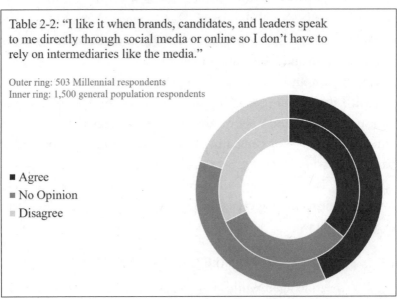

Table 2-2: "I like it when brands, candidates, and leaders speak to me directly through social media or online so I don't have to rely on intermediaries like the media."

Outer ring: 503 Millennial respondents
Inner ring: 1,500 general population respondents

■ Agree
■ No Opinion
■ Disagree

managing director of the global advertising firm R/GA, what is wonderful about video is that it "isn't reliant on written or spoken words to tell an affecting story."[26] Video, and especially live video, is the next best thing to being face-to-face; it is close to being "the ultimate form of engagement."

Livestreaming has the power to change the way your customers see you. It can help build trust and foster a stronger relationship. Communication with your customers no longer needs to be a one-way street of websites, TV and print ads, press releases, and email announcements. Communicating with your customers can become a conversation, with the potential of more nuance and better understanding than is possible with the written word. Livestreaming can bring you closer to your customers and create the kind of lasting experiences that build credibility and strengthen the bonds of trust. Once you use it and get comfortable with it, you will never go back.

WHAT DOES THE DATA TELL US?

It's not a simple thing to clinically capture the appeal and power of unscripted in the data, but from what we've seen, we can triangulate it.

If you ask consumers whether they prefer professionally produced communications from brands or whether they prefer unscripted, livestreaming communications, they much prefer the latter (59 percent).

As to the public preferring to hear directly from leaders through social media, those who want this direct access edge out those who don't, but when we look to Millennials, preference jumps to a 2:1 edge. The future belongs to unscripted.

KEY TAKEAWAYS

What key lessons can we take away from what we have learned? How can we apply them in our own organizations?

How can we use an unscripted approach to foster consumer and employee trust?

In a jaded world, we yearn for the truth. The honesty that comes from an unscripted moment is something we value greatly. We are drawn to leaders who are not afraid of making mistakes and who are willing to show us their imperfections. This way of communicating indicates to us that they are probably telling the truth, and that's what we relate to most.

We are drawn to unscripted leaders because we sense that they know who they are. They are comfortable in their own skin. In a world of fake sincerity and fake news, being unscripted is like a breath of fresh air.

The more opportunities you have to have open conversations with your employees, the greater the chance you can strengthen their trust in you. Therefore, how can you increase the number of occasions you have to listen to your employees, preferably face-to-face? Make a point of spending as much time as possible meeting with your employees one-on-one and in small groups. Spend time listening to what they have to say about your customers and what they like and don't like about their jobs. Listen hard and take their concerns seriously. If you do, they will open up to you and, over time, begin to model your behavior. On the day your employees ask to have a selfie taken with you, you will know that you are getting through to them; you have gained their trust.

How can an unscripted approach change the way we approach our jobs?

Being unscripted opens us up to the world and invites others in. When leaders go on camera in a livestreaming event or stand before their employees without a script or a PowerPoint presentation, they are being unscripted. Consumers listen intently and employees lean forward because they sense you are not there to sell them but to have a meaningful conversation. When you strip away the spin, you draw people to you. Being unscripted in this way builds rapport and trust.

Think about everything you do during the course of a normal workday and then change the way you approach it. If you spend most of your day at your desk or in your office, make a point of spending an hour or more with employees you don't normally interact with.

Do more listening than talking. Ask more questions and give fewer opinions. Make sure it is a conversation, not just a question-and-answer session. If you do formal presentations to your leadership or to your employees, focus on what you want to say, not the mechanics of the presentation. Speak from the heart, not the PowerPoint presentation. Being unscripted is a leadership style that is hard to beat.

How can we use technology to support an unscripted approach?
In the past, if you wanted to engage with consumers in an unscripted manner, you would have had to do it in person. If you were making changes in your strategic direction and you wanted to make sure everyone was on board—or at least understood why you were doing what you were doing—you would have to travel to your different offices, arrange meetings with all of your employees, and take the time to answer all of their questions. That is an effective way to be unscripted. However, it is also very time consuming.

Today there is another way—livestreaming. Livestreaming, like its in-person counterpart, is immediate, candid, personal, and authentic. It allows you to connect directly with consumers using a technology that has become available only in the past few years. There are various ways to use livestreaming: live question-and-answer sessions, at events and product launches, as an interactive series, for company town hall meetings, for panel discussions, and for behind-the-scenes looks at your company's operations. Begin to use livestreaming because, by its very nature, it has the power to change the way your customers and your employees view you and your relationship with them.

CONCLUSION

Given our reliance on technology and the ease with which digital manipulation and "spin" can distort the truth, what emerges as the most credible and honest is unscripted communication, direct from the source. The more personal and direct we can be, the better.

By being unscripted and engaging in direct interactions, we forge a completely new brand experience with our customers. Either in person or via livestreaming, adopting an unscripted approach creates a more human and credible connection. It radically changes the traditional "canned" communications media to a more human form of outreach, and it shifts the culture away from rings of gatekeepers to one where the right people are readily accessible to customers and employees. From a leadership perspective, it is a game-changer.

CHAPTER 3

Rule #3: Raw Means In-Process

*I think we ultimately see a model where we want to empower
creators outside of the brand to create . . . and the resulting network effect there is super exciting. It increasingly gets
towards co-creation and turning the co-creation loose on the
marketplace.*

Paul Gaudio, adidas global creative director, in an
interview with the author on March 20, 2019

When adidas thinks of raw, it thinks of how it can immerse itself
in the culture—sports culture, music culture, fashion culture, and
everything that swirls around this vibrant lifestyle ecosystem—so
that it not only exposes the company's internal culture to outsiders
but also teaches these same outsiders how to influence the internal
culture. The result, as Gaudio goes on to mention, is magic: if you
can teach your team to operate in a constant state of rawness, figura-
tively "swimming in the culture," you end up with results that could
never have happened if you had never left the office.

This second animation of raw is in-process, which, along with
unscripted and in-context, forms the three definitions of raw we're
exploring.

In-process means that technologically immersed consumers demand to be treated as equals, being involved in the process of creation and development, either actively or passively. We want to be

insiders. We're no longer content to be spoon-fed new products that appear fully formed in a splashy launch event. We want our voices heard—from the beginning, if at all possible, but certainly as the design unfolds and reaches the launch phase.

Regardless of whether this means that we've actually been invited into the studio to help design a product or whether we follow the brand on social media and can see, with our own eyes, what a day in the life of a major celebrity looks like, we're participating in the brand experience in a way that would have been unthinkable a decade ago. But today, armed with smartphones, social media, and mobile connectivity, we can, and therefore, like all adoption of new technology, once it's possible, it becomes our expectation. "If I can customize my shoes, I will." "If I can see videos taken by Lebron James in the locker room, I expect to have access to the gestalt of post-game celebration." "If I can come along behind the velvet curtain and see what Cristiano Ronaldo sees when he's prepping for a game, I expect that I'll see more of this experience—because I follow him, and that's what we expect on the socials I use."

This is the present—and near-term future—of fandom. In-process means we're involved every step of the way.

What are the drivers for this desire to be involved in the process? It's helpful to examine these levers to better understand how to replicate them for our own purposes.

The collapse of trust sets the stage for a stronger desire for direct participation in the brand/consumer relationship. If we don't trust the institutions around us—including "big business" or even most of the brands we buy, regardless of sentiment—our opinions are colored by decisions made without our input and consent.

Clearly, having direct access and the ability to have a dialogue with makers via social media has shortened the gap between producer and buyer to a matter of a few electrons. We are technologically able to contribute, or at least participate; therefore, we expect to have the option to do so.

In addition, we can look to the social psychology of interpersonal influence and see how "scarcity" plays into our perceptions as it relates to brand loyalty and preference. If we're invited into the inner sanctum where decisions are made or inputs are provided, we feel like insiders. We can tell our friends we had a hand in things. We can say we knew about this months ago, before the noninsiders heard of it through official channels. And when this happens, we're more likely to support the final product, regardless of whether our input was implemented or not. We were part of it, and therefore we belong.

Moreover, in this age of cynicism, it's critically important that brands not take this approach in a half-hearted way. To commit to the full spirit of cocreation is to push this philosophy deep into the brand's culture so that it goes far beyond a check-the-box "need to have" on a product requirement document, where it resides for many companies today. Our normal functional state today is to be distrustful. Our sense of trust in brands is low. For a brand to truly connect on an authentic level and to achieve a sense of raw in our interactions, we need to not just show up but also constantly communicate this state of being present in everything we do.

This brand/consumer relationship is also deeply rooted in personal technology. We are connected to brands in a deeply personal, real-time way at this point, with our Instagram, Facebook, Twitter, Snapchat, YouTube, and other streams of social media always at our fingertips. We're connected to our network of friends and other loose connections and aren't shy about sharing our impressions, good or bad, at a moment's notice. Impressions and perceptions about how a brand relates to the culture are instantly broadcast and rebroadcast countless times a minute.

Our respect for the native culture around us and our participation in it can't be easily faked when everyone has a camera, a megaphone, and an opinion in their pocket, along with a deeply felt sense of distrust.

With this backdrop in mind, let's explore three ways in-process is animated in the world today, drawing on stories and insights from industry and culture.

First up is a deeper conversation with adidas.

IN-PROCESS AS CULTURAL IMMERSION

For us, it's increasingly about cocreation. I just firmly believe that any time you put people together, especially people from diverse backgrounds or with diverse perspectives, sparks fly and new things happen. You create something that you wouldn't have otherwise created yourself. I think we ultimately see a model where we want to empower creators outside of the brand to create, and that should have a network effect that's super exciting.

Paul Gaudio, adidas global creative chief, in an
interview with the author on March 20, 2019

Gaudio's design philosophy at global sportswear giant adidas signals a departure from legacy thinking that demands all innovation must descend, *deus-ex-machina*-like, from above, from the corporate ivory tower to the rapturous masses of customers passively waiting to buy whatever is put in front of them. The advent of raw means passivity is now passé. We demand to be part of the process now.

Where many brands approach "the voice of the customer" as a step along the path of developing a marketing document, requiring qualitative research or perhaps some end-user inputs along the way, adidas flips the script by doing everything it can to eliminate the boundaries between brand and user.

Beyond the conventional means that most brands rely on for social listening, Gaudio believes that nothing beats first-person, face-to-face contact with the culture. "It's about having our people—all of us—in dialogue with and in contact with the culture," Gaudio says. "In our case, that means sports culture and everything that surrounds it . . . fashion, music, and all these things that sort of emerged over the last decade or so. There's no substitute for contact."

SWIMMING IN THE CULTURE

What does contact mean in this sense? "The most important and most vital thing is to be sure you're swimming in the culture," Gaudio says. "It means we do formal collaborations with a high-profile collaborator that have far-reaching effects, but it also means going to the local high school and playing pick-up basketball, inviting those same kids to the design studio to teach them about how we make what we make and then watch what they do when you give them a little knowledge and power."

Cocreation, in other words, isn't just about collecting inputs and sending members of the select target market back on their way; it's about evangelizing, teaching, and empowering users to step into our shoes while we step into theirs. There's a deeply open, sharing sense of exploration in this process. We are teaching them while they are teaching us.

Involving the external culture in the design process does two things for adidas, starting with protecting themselves from insular thinking. "Something magical happens in those moments when we give people the tools to create with us. Because it will be something new and different, obviously, because of the perspectives that they bring to the table, and that applies to everybody. We're bringing in artists to help us create, we're bringing in athletes to help us create, even kids." This protection against groupthink is particularly important in fashion and athletic wear, where designers often move from one brand to another, and designs, predictably, can begin to look the same.

Second, this collaborative design process also creates more evangelists and rabid fans. "People are so fascinated by what we do; they're so emotionally connected to the brand," Gaudio explains. "We want to pull the curtain back and show them the inner workings.

It changes the relationship with people, bringing them in, bringing them to a level that they're comfortable contributing and feeling like, yeah, what I'm going to do here matters. Consumers today, kids, in particular, are way more comfortable with that."

COCREATION AS CULTURAL CATALYST

The impact on the brand is equally fascinating to consider. We can't institutionalize involving the external culture without fundamentally changing the internal culture of the company. "Our model is very different than the fashion house, you know, where they've got a celebrity creative director, and they've designated themselves as the tastemakers who come up with what is coming for this season," Gaudio says. "We, we like to get dirty, and kind of mix it up and, and mash it up and look for those collisions and the unexpected insights. Our creative mantra is, 'Borne from culture, built for purpose, and daringly simple.' So, borne from culture is the very first step in any process, anything that creates."

The irony isn't lost on us that in an age of technological immersion, where the iconic image of this time and culture is a Generation Z kid with their face buried in a smartphone, adidas stresses the critical importance of human connection, of face-to-face and often nonverbal communication. "Go to a high school football game on a Friday night," Gaudio says. "You don't even need to talk to people; you can just, you know, feel it. You're in the middle of it."

Developing an anthropologist's sense for observation *in situ* is an output of "swimming in the culture," where the observer knows enough to separate the signal from the noise.

IN-PROCESS AS ECOSYSTEM

We're using the channel to build a better brand, period. We're using the channel to actually involve the customer in ways she's never been allowed or invited to become involved [in order] to build an incredibly inclusive movement like a better, more modern brand . . . [1]

Emily Weiss, founder and CEO of Glossier

The preceding example with adidas shows us a powerful story about a well-established brand that takes great effort in diving into the culture to mine out not just insights but also creative direction and execution. When we take our products—ones that are deeply embedded in the culture to begin with—and share them, their design process, and the means to create with core users, "the magic happens," as Gaudio explained.

But what would happen if we started the other way around? What happens when a brand begins life in the culture—and technology—and grows a product line from there?

That's the unique story that Glossier tells us, the "unicorn" direct-to-consumer beauty brand that has, as of this writing, breached a $1 billion valuation on sales of over $100 million.

To tell this story correctly, we need to start with the blog—*IntotheGloss.com*—that Weiss launched in 2010 as a means to share insights and stories of beauty tips, routines, and products from her vantage point as an industry insider at companies like Ralph Lauren, *Vogue*, and other brands in the cultural bull's-eye of young consumers and beauty. The blog struck a nerve, to say the least, amassing over 10 million readers a month and tapping into an unmet, emerging hunger for understated, almost-not-there beauty products for consumers who loved the idea of feeling good about themselves, rather than insecure about their appearances. This nexus of emerging trends and an audience looking for something better led to the launch of physical, tangible products.

"It was never a pivot," Weiss said of the move from the blog to the launch of physical products. "(It) was a total evolution of the same mission, but with *tactile content.*"[2]

How does this publishing platform as physical product brand come together? The first notable product the company produced through crowd-sourced inspiration began as a simple question on the blog, probing the shortcomings of face cleansers, titled "What's Your Dream Cleanser?" This post garnered several hundred comments and suggestions, leading the company to launch its Milky Jelly cleanser product a year later in 2016. A similar process produced a sunscreen product in 2017.

Beyond the blog, the brand is heavily invested in both social and real-life listening. Its Instagram presence has over a million followers, and the company actively solicits real human contact with fans and users in events designed to be social first, business second.

The ability to leverage an entire ecosystem—and at 10 million readers a month, the proper definition might be an entire population—for insight, product definition and development, competitive intelligence, not to mention publicity, is an eye-opening idea for any brand. How many brands today, particularly those that sell physical products, consider themselves "platforms" rather than "supply chains"? How many brands today are production-oriented, focused more on factory fill rates, rather than consumer—or even just "fan"—oriented? This is an enormous cultural shift in perspective for any company and one that may well be impossible for those who come from non-start-up environments. This isn't the sort of strategy that can be bolted on after hearing a keynote speech or reading an article, because the prototypical corporate behemoth most in need of this sort of cultural shift would surround this idea and kill it like so many organizational white blood cells. But that's the point, isn't it? This is the sort of thinking that ensures "in-process" can be properly leveraged. No one ever lost because they were too close to the customer.

In a very real sense, Weiss and her vision for Glossier seek to create something bigger than the brand. And this is very often a path to explosive growth beyond the narrow confines of the category you find yourself in. "We're using the channel to build a better brand, period," Weiss says. "We're using the channel to actually involve the customer in ways she's never been allowed or invited to become involved . . . to build an incredibly inclusive movement like a better, more modern brand, which is going become default."[3]

Create a movement first, in other words, and the brand (and revenue) will follow.

IN-PROCESS AS IN-THE-MOMENT AND
THE EXPLOSION OF LIVE MUSIC

One of the few bright spots in the music business is live music, driven in large part by the "you had to be there" dynamic . . . the strong appeal of the fan's direct, unfiltered connection with an artist and the no Auto-Tune, no soft lens, no sleek industrial veneer . . . just the performer and their art.

Paul Schomer, president of MicroSessions, in an
interview with the author on March 28, 2019

We can appreciate adidas and Glossier as two examples of the intersection of culture and commerce—one, a seventy-year-old brand with a heritage of cultural immersion; the other, a brand less than a decade old that emerged from the culture itself—both extraordinary case studies of in-process cocreation, both breathing the air of the culture to continue their respective journeys.

We see a third way here in describing the broader picture of in-process, and the lesson emerges not from a brand case study but from a cultural movement. The ability for a brand—or an artist—to create an experience, an event, where everyone involved is fully engaged and participating in some small (or large) way in its unfolding is worth exploring so we can distill some meaning out of it. Because it's big. And it's growing.

As Millennials point their increasing purchasing power toward acquiring experiences rather than material possessions, we see an increasing hunger for the endorphin rush of unique, raw experiences—live events—that embrace cocreation in the moment and become meaningful not for their lack of flaws but because of them. Being live means there's no possibility of post-production or Auto-Tune covering up mistakes, which is the whole point. You're there, in the moment, accepting what comes and participating physically and emotionally in the outcome.

The numbers certainly support this movement. While the physical purchasing of music is down in double digits over the last twelve months, live music is now projected to reach $30 billion globally in the next several years into the mid 2020s, from live concerts to festivals to small-scale clubs and events. This is not just a provincial American phenomenon, either, with major festival sponsors leveraging their learnings from US and European roots to expand their reach into South America, Asia, and Africa.

People want to experience unique moments, and live events are where these experiences happen. And, as Paul Schomer, the president of small venue "speed dating for music events" provider MicroSessions tells us, a lot of the appeal comes from the unfiltered, in-the-moment, you-had-to-be-there nature of seeing it live.

"Promoters are laser-focused, pushing the connection with the artist, with the ultimate goal being to convince fans that they're an integral part of the show." MicroSessions itself is a product of this raw experience, with Schomer bringing both established and relatively undiscovered artists from different genres together in a house concert-type setting, giving attendees an up-close experience of four artists or so in an evening. From its home base in Austin, Texas, MicroSessions has expanded to New York, San Antonio, and Washington, DC, leveraging this trend of raw in-process experience.

This desire to push the boundaries of unique experience goes well beyond up-and-coming artists to include some of the biggest names in music. Many headliners are looking to create unique, more intimate concerts and face-to-face experiences in nontraditional venues that leverage intimacy and exclusivity. Locations are secret and acts only revealed the day of a show, unorthodox presentation formats are tested, and emerging multisensory technology is trialed. Roc Nation artist Rihanna launched her 2015 single "BBHMM" to eighty trusting fans who signed up on streaming service TIDAL for a vaguely described exclusive event in Los Angeles. They assembled at a location and were then blindfolded, put on a luxury coach, and whisked to an exclusive venue where the artist unveiled her new video and spent the rest of the evening partying with her fans. The event was heavily covered in social media and by the fans on-site, with the new single and album exclusively streamed by the sponsoring TIDAL.

This event gives us a unique lens on how an artist can create a series of concentric rings of exclusivity: the eighty people who attended the launch event, their network of friends and contacts, all the way to the artist's fans on TIDAL who never even heard of the event but could still stream the new single—all come together to create a tight ecosystem of exclusivity and face-to-face experience with the sort of celebrity most fans would never encounter in such a unique setting. This represents nothing less than a systematic, planned shock to the system of fans already taken out of their environment and put in a highly controlled but still uncertain situation (they were blindfolded, after all) in anticipation of something utterly unique.

And this shock to the system is perhaps the point: we're looking for raw experience and want to be part of the performance, so this is a necessary step. Is this a response to already overstimulated minds with access to every possible experience under the sun by virtue of an internet connection? Are we so starved for novelty that the hunger for a shock to the system drives us to seek out more extreme experiences? Against the adrenaline-rush-junkie subculture, looking for raw experience in live music may seem tame. This isn't a bad thing. But it may signal a step down this path for the nonzealot looking for "the shock of raw."

Another angle to consider is a trend from previous studies, one we've called "The Pursuit of Nextness"—the desire to not just be content with experiencing an event first-hand but also being the first to share it. "It's like everyone is now a reporter, and they're all there to capture pictures and video in the moment," Jennifer Sullivan, president of entertainment marketing agency memBrain explained in an April 10, 2019, interview with us. "You go to these festivals, and it's just a sea of phones. It's not that they're necessarily there to commune with the other people there . . . they're there to commune with the rest of the world and with people at home on their couches." Consider that once upon a time, concertgoers would collect ticket stubs as their "proof of legitimacy." Now, they collect metadata.

The preceding example is merely a stepping-off point. Tiered pricing and VIP experiences are becoming mainstream, with varying degrees of up-sell opportunities for pre- or postshow meet-and-greets with the artists, tour sponsor product or service tie-ins, exclusive artist downloads, and more all on sale.

Don't expect things to stop here, either. As the public pushes for more such shocks to the system while looking for opportunities to be part of the performance, technology will help fill the gap both in terms of scale as well as in augmenting the immersive experience. What's coming next? "The last frontier of innovation, of course, blends technology with the live show," Schomer explains. "While live video streaming of concerts has yet to really take hold here in the West, Asia has fully embraced the concept, with free and pay-per-view live shows engaging audience numbers in the hundreds of thousands and even millions for the most popular acts. Musicians in Asia get tipped in the form of virtual currency, e-gifts or e-flowers exchanged for cash by the fans. The revenue potential is massive—imagine if professional basketball players made no salary and just got tipped by thousands of fans every time they made a three-pointer, blocked a shot, or hit a free throw?"

We may be living in a digitally immersed world today, but more and more we see examples of a rebalancing, of a rehumanizing of experience, as we do here. This doesn't mean digital experiences have no place in this emerging live ecosystem; digital will always have a significant role by virtue of the fact that we're still culturally plugged into our digital footprints via social media and mobile devices during all of our waking hours. But we're seeing too many examples of digital becoming an overlay to the human connection to quickly pass it off. There's definitely something here, and it bears studying.

WHAT DOES THE DATA TELL US?

We've looked at several key questions relating to the hunger for cocreation, in-process communication, and the search for raw experience over the past four surveys we've conducted. When we probe attitudes toward whether US respondents would prefer brands to keep details to themselves and present their final product in a big launch event or whether they would prefer frequent communication and in-process codevelopment as the product is developed so that the launch event signals more of a first ship date rather than an unveiling, responses in the US, across all groups, are very stable—roughly three-quarters of respondents prefer knowing what's coming, participating in the process, and being some sort of insider in the development phase as opposed to being the passive recipient of other people's work.

Our data over the past two years supports this sentiment across the globe as well. In China, those supporting frequent contact and collaboration are closer to 80 percent versus "big unveilers." Both Germany and Japan are in the mid-70 percent range. Of the countries surveyed over this period of time, the UK showed the weakest interest in supporting a more open product development process, and yet Britain still has roughly two-thirds supporting it. Call it a global phenomenon. Sentiment is uniformly in favor of more communication, in-process check-ins, and codevelopment.

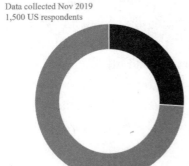

Table 3-1: "When you think of how a favorite brand communicates with you when launching a new product, which would you prefer?"

Data collected Nov 2019
1,500 US respondents

■ "The brand builds up the suspense, announcing everything at once, making the launch a big event with lots of publicity and surprise."

■ "The brand communicates frequently, collecting input from customers and showng work in progress, so you know what's coming before it's finally revealed."

The question of a preference for live (versus prerecorded) performance, on the other hand, shows significant nuance. Overall, 43 percent of American respondents said they prefer live performance over prerecorded ones, with 31 percent disagreeing. When we split this by gender, male respondents report a 55 percent preference versus 33 percent for females. Millennials, too, show a strong preference for live, with 53 percent in favor. We even saw an interesting skew in political persuasion here, as well, with 61 percent of self-described "very conservatives" preferring live performance versus 45 percent self-described "very liberal" respondents. Seeing a performance as it happens is more compelling, perhaps because the outcome is unclear, and we're all experiencing the event together (at least at the same time, if not in the same place). Perhaps we value live performance because of the pressure put on the participants, and perhaps we watch because we want to see the mistakes, because acknowledging the flaws and forgiving them make us all equally human. But clearly, we can agree that with live viewing, there is no room for airbrushing the mistakes out before they're caught. Live is inherently more believable because it's harder to lie when it's all happening in real time.

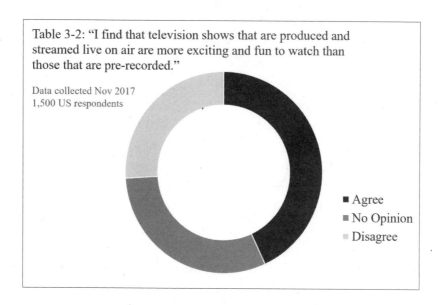

Table 3-2: "I find that television shows that are produced and streamed live on air are more exciting and fun to watch than those that are pre-recorded."

Data collected Nov 2017
1,500 US respondents

■ Agree
■ No Opinion
■ Disagree

KEY TAKEAWAYS

Given what we've learned, how do we put these lessons to use? Here are the key takeaways and somewhat rhetorical questions we have to consider to get the most out of these insights.

How can we shift corporate cultures that are so often based on secrecy and "need to know" to a place where cocreation can systematically happen?

If our corporate cultures are based on secrecy, with a deep fear of letting outsiders have a look at our processes and methods, cocreation can be a tough sell. Lawyers write nondisclosures and have templates drafted that say that any idea submitted to the company will be thrown away unread or that no outside ideas will be accepted, and thus, no compensation now or in the future will be paid, etc. We've all seen this. And it's OK! There's nothing wrong with this legal or cultural stance. However, if we're to tap this tremendous opportunity and reap the benefits of cultural immersion and cocreation, we need to carve out a place where this becomes possible. So craft up the right legal agreements. Keep your top-secret parts top secret. But find ways, even at the edges at first if that's what's available to you, to pilot this idea. Results create opportunities for more funding and attention. Start somewhere.

What institutionalized listening policies do we need to establish to fully leverage an in-process philosophy across the enterprise?

Few companies take this issue as seriously as they should, and many don't even have rudimentary listening processes in place, let alone resources, either in-house or outsourced, to handle it. The key question is how can we create a listening culture—and observational culture—that can coexist within our own? What simple tools can we use in the course of our daily roles that can bring in the element of customer real-time feedback and commentary? On the simplest level, this entails little more than a properly set up social listening platform to gather brand references that can be quickly synthesized. Such listening platforms extend upward into most major marketing automation platforms today, for those further up the ladder. In those cases where deep cultural dives are desired to understand more complex phenomena, the budding field of cultural online ethnography—*netnography*, as coined and originated by University of Southern California professor Robert Kozinets—is a more sophisticated and specialized approach. But in each case, the ability to institutionalize sentiment and feedback from the culture itself is the end result. How you apply it within your own organizational culture is up to you.

What cultural changes do we need to make in order to fully immerse our design, product management, marketing, and other customer-facing groups in the culture?

When Paul Gaudio of adidas says his team is "swimming in the culture," he means they are immersed in cultural insight, living and breathing it on a daily basis. This isn't something that a product manager dips into once a quarter. This isn't a question of doing focus groups once a year. This is a total shift in mindset that says we will always be in a state of engagement with our users, our customers, our market, and our culture. Meetings and discussions should all flow around anecdotes, data, video clips, and other evidence of first-person observation. This goes beyond "customer centricity" and suggests something more akin to "customer immersive." Likewise, this is beyond a "facts not feelings" culture; this is evidence plus insight, often to the point that the market itself can't articulate what you have discerned from their actions and appearances. You simply know them better than they know themselves because you're paying closer attention to what they're doing and thinking than they are.

How do we ensure we have the political air cover to systematically reinvent ourselves—to question all the givens in our industry and to see ourselves with beginners' eyes?

Every CEO in the world embraces this idea in the abstract, but far fewer are willing to put resources behind it to see it happen. The management team that dedicates smart people—insiders as well as chosen outsiders—to create strategies that would undermine all of the company's well-laid plans is rare but well prepared. The same goes for cultural immersion. What resources can you bring to the fight to create a product that throws out all the normal expectations? Who can you bring in from the outside to help you see your business with beginners' eyes? How can you best employ strategic naivety and let your market design your product—right down to the kid on the high school blacktop or the long-time knowledge worker who is just an expert in their own world?

How can we take the art of creative collaboration to its illogical extreme?

Mash-ups, collaborations, and other collisions of genre and style can be magical—in music, food, art, and probably in your business, too. The magic always happens on the edges. How can you creatively bring in talented outsiders from different disciplines to cocreate your next big idea? How can their insights—and their brand halo effect—impact your business? How would partnering with a different industry segment in a different walk of life change not just a jointly developed product but also how your brand is perceived in the world?

What would we do with 10 million readers visiting our company blog each month? What would we ask them, how would we synthesize their inputs, and how would we go about building this army of followers?

Let's continue the preceding idea for a moment. What if you had 10 million—or 10,000, for that matter—active visitors coming to your company blog each month, responding to your daily posts, talking to each other, and providing daily insights and inputs? The blog would serve as more than just a publicity medium. It would be a product development forum, a competitive intelligence source, a marketing launch vehicle, and a lot more. What steps can you take to build up your platform, and how can you turn a "newsletter" into a communications medium augmented by smart segmentation, direct feedback, and human connection?

How can we give our audience the "in-arena experience," pushing them out of their passive comfort zones?

The growth of live events isn't limited to the music scene. Many brands are realizing that in a digital whiteout, where there's too much noise coming across your customer's smartphone, the best way to reach your market isn't by yelling louder—it's by being where they physically are and talking to them when their mindset is in a more receptive mood. Namely, when they're off the couch, away from their office, and on their feet, preferably having fun. But there's more to it than just venue. How do we create experiences that put people in a receptive mindset? We don't need to take this to an extreme; there's no need to put them on stage doing improv, if that's not their thing. But breaking the normal patterns of behavior and getting people in a different social setting where they're getting welcome stimuli that's decidedly not the ordinary business experience works. Find a whiteboard and start coming up with ways to create a different experience for them.

CONCLUSION

Technology and culture are moving in symbiotic ways, with each teaching the other how to best get the most out of the relationship. In-process illustrates how we, as users, *want* to be part of the process because we *can* be part of the process—by virtue of our technologically connected lives and our interest in frequent communication from the brands we care about. We have a desire for inclusion. We want to be included because it connects us personally, exclusively, to the outcome where an outsider would feel no personal connection at all. This is a deeply personal phenomenon that exists only because of how we've evolved to best coexist with the technology we've come to rely on.

CHAPTER 4

Rule #4: Raw Means In-Context

I don't think consumers want a completely unmediated experience because they won't know what's going on. Unmediated footage is just chaotic. The real responsibility of a broadcaster is context—to put it all in a framework that allows for understanding.

Rob Sharenow, president of programming
for A&E Networks, in an interview
with the author on October 25, 2019

Information has always been a scarce commodity, at least up until about twenty years ago.

From the time of the Gutenberg printing press to the very recent past, information has been available only to the rare few with the skills or access to acquire it. As technology has emerged as a cultural driver, it has given everyday people the tools to create and disseminate content on every possible subject. There are pros and cons that come along with this development, to be sure. We now have first-person viewpoints on major historical events, with video showing us what is actually happening in Tahrir Square or Bangkok or just at a local political rally or baseball game. We can see with our own eyes whether the news is telling us the truth—or can we? Not every citizen journalist is publishing their video content without bias. What may look to the casual observer to be police brutality may not fully tell the story, particularly when the first thirty seconds have been edited out.

A&E Networks' *Live PD* has made a resounding impact on the American cultural conversation in this arena. Given the extreme interest in understanding what is really happening on the street between communities and law enforcement, *Live PD* has stepped into a volatile situation in an effort to simply provide context—showing the viewing audience what is actually happening, while it is actually happening, and then providing an expert education on what the viewer is actually seeing. *Live PD* is as close to livestreaming as possible, allowing viewers to see not the postproduction clean-up of an event, but the chases and confrontations as they happen on American streets across the country.

In-context is the last of the three definitions of raw that we're exploring, which, together with unscripted and in-process, provides a well-rounded understanding of how smart brands and practitioners are navigating this important shift in sentiment.

In-context means we want to understand the backstory before we choose to trust. We want to understand why things are the way they are, to understand the history, the rules, the pedigree, the probabilities that underpin what we're asked to accept. If we can teach our audience how to best interpret what they're seeing so they're more expert than they were before, we can rely on their own judgment to come to the right decisions with some confidence. We're no longer just lecturing our audience; we're giving them the context behind our thinking so they can make up their own minds.

In-context tempers the chaos of unmediated, raw information and teaches our viewers how to interpret what they're seeing. Now that we're seeing a maturing of livestreaming as a medium, the additional layer of context becomes critically important.

Against a backdrop of marketing in general being perceived as a negative, zero-sum proposition, context allows us to step out of our old role of seller and adopt a newer and more acceptable role as teacher, educating our audience without the implied win/lose back-drop. When we teach our audience how to better understand complex phenomena—be it applying a B2B solution to an enterprise's technology stack, or educating a salesforce on how a new market entrant fits in an already-crowded market's ecosystem, or simply understanding police work so the audience can see what officers are subjected to on a nightly basis—we essentially move our audience down the path to becoming experts. And experts become evangelists who tell others.

There's a dire need for context in this new age of super-abundant video because what we see isn't always what it appears to be. From citizen journalists with dubious credentials and questionable motives posting video on Facebook to truly photo-realistic deep fakes, truth has become subjective.

An absolute raw feed gives us the experience of real life. But without context, do we really know what we're seeing?

TAKING THE SUBJECTIVITY OUT OF EMOTIONALLY CHARGED SOCIAL ISSUES

There is a hunger for understanding the human condition, particularly the parts that we don't necessarily participate in on a daily basis, where the ability to don a separate persona, even for an hour, is appealing. We want the experience of life in as vivid a manner as possible, without having to live through the consequences ourselves.

That's probably as good a reason as any to point to the success of A&E Networks' hit show *Live PD*. The combination of six livestreaming feeds of real-time law enforcement on American streets and the expert analysis by the show's panel provides us with real-time, first-person perspective on one of America's most controversial and tension-fraught issues, putting us in the shoes of front-line law enforcement officers. But seeing an incident live isn't the same as understanding what we're seeing. Without the expertise to judge each night's many highly charged incidents, we'd just be witnessing chaos, as A&E Networks president of programming, Rob Share-now, explains.

"There's a certain amount of sophistication now about nonfiction video, and there's a high level of skepticism and a nuanced under-standing of how things are put together, so much so that there's a demand for more transparency and things that are unassailably authentic," Sharenow tells us. "Back in the day, we had such limited exposure to images of the real world that we didn't have much to compare it to. Now, the gloves have come off. But it's led to a certain level of skepticism about documentary and news content, and that's a challenge."

A&E has made the conscious decision to push the envelope as far as possible in capturing a certain type of intense documentary storytelling that strives for an unfiltered, raw feeling. In the case of *Live PD*, the fit was certainly there, although there was a concern that production would be difficult to manage. First, the technolog-ical aspects of six live feeds happening simultaneously, all on the same night, created a significant challenge. On the more human side, Sharenow was convinced that he'd have trouble getting police departments to cooperate, despite what the production company promised him. Fortunately, his concerns on both fronts turned out to be unnecessary. "One of the things that surprised me was the sheer number of police departments that wanted to participate," Sharenow explains. "The more that's going on, the more they want the third-party cameras there to bear witness to what's happening out there."

Clearly, though, there's more to this approach than just showing an audience the raw feed. The point about chaos is correct. Real life, on screen, is dull and confusing. We need help in understanding what we're seeing. "Viewers want a rich experience," Sharenow con-cludes. "They want to know what's going on. And that's part of the problem in an increasingly unmediated digital age, that there's so much out there that's unexplained, so context is valuable."

CREATING COMMON GROUND FOR A DIVIDED CULTURE

The issue of trust and the way each viewer interprets their own version of seeking control in an out-of-control world is important to reflect on here, while we're discussing *Live PD*. The polarization of the current American mindset deserves more attention than we can properly give it in this book, but within the context of *Live PD*, we see different communities relating strongly to different sides within the show. "I think what's fascinating is people interpret *Live PD* differently depending on where they fit in with what they're seeing," Sharenow says. "Some people are sympathetic to the cops. Some people are less sympathetic to the cops and more sympathetic to the perpetrators. What I find very interesting is that we're still living in the same moment where trust and facts are being questioned on all sides, so it does speak to the point that whoever watches the show believes they're seeing something authentic and real . . . and then there's just a difference of opinion about what people think about it."

Regardless of our opinions on the more subjective nature of what we're viewing, in other words, we accept the evidence at face value. It's hard to casually dismiss live video of someone running from a traffic stop and excuse that behavior. It's harder still to align everyone—from the community to law enforcement—on whether the police are in the right to patrol and enforce the laws the way they do. Your opinions may vary.

THE CHAOS OF CHOICE

It's important to revisit a key element of *Live PD* and bring it back to what we, as brand stewards, can control. When bandwidth and storage are essentially free and the barriers to content creation are nonexistent, we run the risk of providing not context to our customers but confusion. "The problem we're facing now is the chaos of choice," Sharenow says. "There's so much content and there's so many platforms, it's like a cacophony." Marketers run the risk of drowning our audiences in content in the hope that viewers will somehow parse through the sea of information we've given them and find the truth on their own, but this is a dangerous assumption and one we should avoid. As information on every possible topic has come online and thus available to anyone with a browser, we might also venture to guess that our intellectual curiosity as a culture has shrunk almost as much as our collective attention spans.

And what of trust? What of our own natural biases when it comes to what we choose to provide as context and what we choose to leave out? How do we address this issue in a responsible and ethical manner? Our answer goes back to the very basis of this entire discussion. This shift to raw—of an unscripted, in-process, and in-context approach to information—is how we address this shortfall of trust. If we can simply present the evidence—showing the video of the car chase and then describing what the law is on the matter—we can all agree on the basic issue of whether we're telling the truth or not. We can argue later over motivations and mitigating factors.

Sharenow mirrors this view regarding trust and describes a viable next step—one that suggests a pendulum swing back toward how things were before the rise of citizen journalists, with a twist. "I think that the demand for curation will emerge," Sharenow says. "I think that's something no one's really talking about right now. I think consumers like to have organizing principles and curation of their content. Otherwise, it's just too much for people to manage or deal with. We're coming to a point where there's so much good, but there's also a tremendous amount of bad that people don't want to have to sift through."

We need to help our customers connect the dots, in other words. It's not that they're stupid; it's that they're busy, distracted, and largely indifferent to our goals as marketers. As such, we need to make decisions about how to provide context—to frame up what is educational and what is noise.

IN-CONTEXT AND PREACHING TO THE ALREADY-CONVERTED

Consumers want to know where their food comes from. And we want to be able to help inform them.

Mike Helgeson, former CEO of Gold'n Plump Poultry, in an interview with the author on October 22, 2019

Rob Sharenow's experiences running *Live PD* provide a case study in visual context—of showing the evidence and, importantly, stopping to provide the necessary backstory to teach us how to interpret what we're seeing. We may have our own biases going into the experience. We may automatically side with law enforcement or with the community they police. But if the evidence is clearly presented, at least we don't have to argue over whether we're seeing the truth.

In this spirit, let's start with the assumption that we're working with an audience that already has a clear bias, possibly a firmly stated desire to espouse a social or political position or a lifestyle goal they're looking to support. What if we just cater our marketing messaging—and our product development, logistic supply chain, and entire corporate philosophy dating back nearly a hundred years—to a specific segment of the market that strongly believes in something as natural as "eating locally grown food"?

If this sounds like you or someone you know, you're not alone! Increasingly, we care—sometimes deeply—about where our food comes from, how it was raised or farmed, and how it was transported, right down to the name of the farmer responsible for the chicken on our dinner table. This new approach to food began in the mid-1980s with the "slow food" movement springing up in Italy and continuing into the early years of the 2000s with the "locavore" movement beginning in San Francisco. The greater interest and concern over factory farming, the humane treatment of animals in the food supply, the use of antibiotics, and the general concern for the environment all fueled this shift in public sentiment.

THE MID-2000S—A TURNING POINT FOR BOTH
FOOD CULTURE AND TECHNOLOGY

It's interesting to look at the mid-decade period of the early 2000s and understand the different forces that emerged during this time. The year 2005 saw the birth of the locavore movement, followed two years later by it being crowned as the "Word of the Year" by the *New Oxford American Dictionary*. In 2006, Michael Pollan's seminal work, *The Omnivore's Dilemma*, was published, describing for many new readers exactly what went into the food they ate on a daily basis. And, not for nothing, the iPhone launched in 2007, creating the means by which movements like these were able to take root and organically grow much faster, thanks to the rise of mobile social networks, video capture and instant publication, and everything that came with the smartphone era.

In the midst of all this, Mike Helgeson—the now former CEO of Gold'n Plump Poultry, a brand that grew out of his grandfather's seasonal hatchery that dated back to 1926—saw the opportunity to take what was already considered to be a premium food brand and further embrace the building social wave behind the "know your farmer" movement. Just before this epochal decade of the 2000s came to a close, Gold'n Plump launched its Just BARE line of fresh poultry, aimed squarely at the emerging market for "mindful eaters."

Just BARE was one of the first food brands to educate consumers at the supermarket on exactly where their chicken came from, right down to the farm. "With the mindful eater segment, it was even more important for them to know where their food was coming from," Helgeson says. "We were one of the first companies to let consumers enter the product code on the packaging and that would let you trace it back to one grower. Part of it was people wanted to know where their food was coming from. Part of it, especially for the mindful eater category, was that they were concerned about how the product was raised too."

THE PSYCHOLOGY OF CHOICE

Why this interest in tracing the sources of what goes into the goods we buy? We can point to a number of potential triggers for this shift in sentiment. The sheer explosion of brand choices available to consumers drives a good bit of this movement, as consumers need ways to understand for themselves what makes one brand different from another. The move to localization itself and the support for small business drive this, as well, as we look to smaller, more underdog-type brands that we more closely identify with on a personal level. Brands, too, have a need to embrace their roots as origin stories and storytelling in general rise to the fore in the minds of consumers. Being able to trace your food back to a specific place and grown by a specific person—with a name and a face—is a dramatic change from the anonymous origins of most national brands. And while technology itself is the means by which we learn and share these unique stories with our networks of friends, this trend is also likely a pendulum swing away from lives that are immersed in technology. What better antidote to digital overload than a farmer's market, where you meet the people who grew your food?

In a sense, we can define traceability as the sum of transparency plus storytelling, giving us the visibility into the origins of the product we buy and also breathing life into it so that it has greater meaning. We'd be remiss if we didn't also give a nod toward the ability of the consumer to retell these stories, as they help bolster our own sense of self. We identify with the brands we buy—even if they're "unbranded" in the more usual sense of the word. We also also need to note that the transparency and availability of the contextual information are important, regardless of whether we as consumers choose to look them up or not. The fact that the transparency is there plays a big role in its believability. "Consumers want to know where their food comes from," Helgeson says. "And we want to be able to help inform them. We thought it would be important to give consumers the tools to trace their product back if they wanted to, and I think it also helped us put a face to the grower, the family having that connection with a family farmer. They want to see where the food comes from and know who is producing it."

HELPING A SKEPTICAL MARKET BELIEVE

Providing full traceability all the way back to the farm and the farmer that produced the food you're buying for your family is an important part of the trust equation, and building this kind of trust is what underpins a powerful, respected brand. But building brand equity and trust takes effort as well as time. In Gold'n Plump's case, the overriding philosophy that has guided this consumer-centric mindset stretches back at least as far as the brand's founding in 1978, with certain elements pointing all the way back to the company's roots in 1926.

"I think our philosophy and our culture of being open and engaging our team members stretches all the way to our goal of providing consumers with the value they're looking for," Helgeson says. The company was the only one in its industry to share profits with its growers, not just its employees. Beyond this, hatcheries that supplied Gold'n Plump with its flocks were paid by the square foot of barn space devoted to raising poultry, even if the barn sat empty. This guaranteed payment system evened out the cash flow issues that many producers have and created a stronger bond with the brand as an ethical partner of choice. The brand's philosophy and ethics rippled outward like a series of concentric circles, from how the company treated its employees to how it treated its growers, eventually making its way to the retailers and consumers themselves. Traceability, in the case of Gold'n Plump, was simply the brand's way of introducing one group of stakeholders to another.

"Over time, consumers wanted to know more about the product they're buying and also more about the company they're buying it from," Helgeson says. "They want to know if the company stood for something. The company's reputation is important. That's one of the reasons we produced the *Farm to Fork Report*, which became a tool to communicate what we're doing. People want to buy from a company that they know and trust. They want to do business with a good steward of the environment and a good community supporter."

CREATING EXPERTS, ONE PICK-AND-ROLL AT A TIME

There will be a day when you look back and say, I can't imagine we all used to watch the same thing at the same time. That seems silly.[1]

Rajiv Maheswaran, CEO of Second Spectrum

Embracing the idea of "in-context" can, as we've shown, help shed light on subjective and highly charged questions in the minds of the public as well as cement a brand's credibility in the eyes of advocates looking for undeniable proof of performance, as *Live PD* and Gold'n Plump clearly illustrate. Both of these animations of in-context build word of mouth and positive brand equity. Both answer questions the public may raise about how you do what you do, and, as such, both are important—particularly in an age of citizen journalists, the social media wolfpack, and outrage culture.

But if our goal is to push our message out into the world and build true engagement, is this idea of in-context enough?

Based on what we've learned, we answer "yes." Here's why.

Experts are more important to your brand than fans are.

Experts have in-depth knowledge and are ready to explain complexity to others. They are passionate because they understand what they're seeing at a deeper level than others and learn to appreciate it themselves more deeply because of their understanding. We all tend to ignore what we don't understand, but deeper knowledge creates passion and interest. You might have walked past a still-life painting in a museum without a second thought—unless you had learned that this particular painting was the first of its kind, showing three-dimensional perspective, thrusting the imperfect and scarred edge of the table toward the viewer, leaving the spots on the fruit and leaves instead of showing a traditionally boring perfect scene (read Peter Robb's excellent *M: The Man Who Became Caravaggio* for the full story). Marketers need to find ways to create experts because experts not only burn with greater passion, but they also tend to teach others. Experts can't help it. They can't be quiet on the subject because knowledge and expertise breed passion. True evangelists are experts. Fans are casual.

The NBA has a lot of fans, but over the past several years, the league has increasingly seen worrying signs. As of late 2019, television viewership has been flat to declining, year after year, since the 2012 season. Part of this is technology's fault, too. It's hard to keep fans riveted to the TV (or whatever device they're watching a game on) when distractions abound. There's social media to contend with. There are other shows on TV, too. There's both at once, to be honest; most people of basketball-watching age are interacting with a minimum of two devices when they're watching televised content. Has technology and distraction doomed televised basketball?

EXPERTS AND ENGAGEMENT

"If you think about people's attention spans, I'm not sure if you were starting from scratch now that you would design a two-and-a-half-hour experience," NBA commissioner Adam Silver says. "But when are we losing people? At commercial breaks? Is halftime too long? Once they're sitting in the stands, you're competing against Snapchat, Instagram, Facebook. . . ."[2]

Into this quandary stepped former Microsoft CEO Steve Ballmer, now owner of the LA Clippers. Ballmer's interest was piqued after spending time learning more about a small LA-based start-up called Second Spectrum, run by Rajiv Maheswaran, that had the contract to provide NBA teams with in-game analytics—analyzing shot selection probability by player, shot location, and a host of other factors that influence success or failure. Ballmer saw a bigger opportunity than just shot probability and analytics aimed at educating the coaching staff; he saw the possibilities of bringing this level of understanding directly to the consumer. This insight led to the birth of the LA Clippers' Court Vision app.

Court Vision is a smartphone app that acts as a second layer of intelligence on top of the actual game livestream you watch on your phone. The app utilizes multiple video feeds, artificial intelligence, and augmented reality to analyze what's happening on the court in real time and then synthesize all this into an improved viewing experience.

Viewers have the choice of watching the game in one of three modes on their smartphone or tablet. In "player mode," viewers can see a dynamic display of shot probability statistics that follow each player on the court in real time, all based on historical analytics of each player's performance over time, given their position on the court. As players move, their individualized probability percentages change; one player's percentage soars as they get closer to the basket while a great three-point shooter's number stays high when they're beyond the arc.

In "coach mode," viewers can see anticipated player movement based on the team's recorded plays diagrammed on screen, teaching them how the team's offense or defense works and what to expect as it happens. If you've ever been totally ignorant of how a professional basketball team runs an offense, "coach mode" will teach you what this side of the game looks like, all while it's actually happening.

And, of course, there's "mascot mode," which provides on-screen cartoon-like animation that follows the action and celebrates baskets with explosions, fireballs, and other callouts, all for the more casual fan watching less for education and more for entertainment. Viewers can shift between modes by swiping across the screen; they can also switch camera angles to view the game from either basket, half-court, or from courtside, where the coaches sit.

CHANGING BEHAVIORS THROUGH MAINSTREAMING ANALYTICS

This "moneyball-ization" of basketball analytics has already shifted the culture in the league. Second Spectrum's CEO, Rajiv Maheswaran, has described the feedback he's received from league players. They say that where once upon a time a coach would instruct them to move the ball to a specific spot on the court because "that's what I said to do," this newly evolved game is now coached by telling players that their shot success will now be "X percent more efficient." Putting these tools in the hands of the consumer—in a radically more consumer-friendly manner, as well—changes not only how viewers watch a game but also how they understand it.

Court Vision brings this concept of creating experts to life in a very tangible way. Many of us in this culture have dribbled a basketball before. Many of us have played at some level, from pick-up games in the neighborhood to recreational leagues. Not as many have taken part in highly organized league or state-level play where we've been taught, hands-on, by a coach what a pick-and-roll is or what a screen looks like. Fewer still have run a sophisticated offense that depends on a series of ball movements, cuts, pick-and-roll moves, and the like. As a result, basketball can seem chaotic and punctuated by individual performers who look to be freelancing for the entirety of the game. Seeing the game the viewer has come to know through a different lens—particularly one that explains complex phenomena in a simple way, in real time—is truly game changing.

"We recognize that we're competing against every other possible form of entertainment," NBA commissioner Adam Silver says. "What can we do to make those games more of a lean-in experience? Providing statistics during the games, providing more information about the players, providing new camera angles, new ways to predict to produce them, augmented reality. . . ."[3] Silver's thinking on this matter—along with Ballmer's and Maheswaran's implementation of

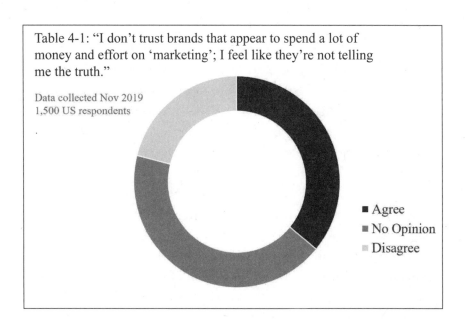

Table 4-1: "I don't trust brands that appear to spend a lot of money and effort on 'marketing'; I feel like they're not telling me the truth."

Data collected Nov 2019
1,500 US respondents

■ Agree
■ No Opinion
■ Disagree

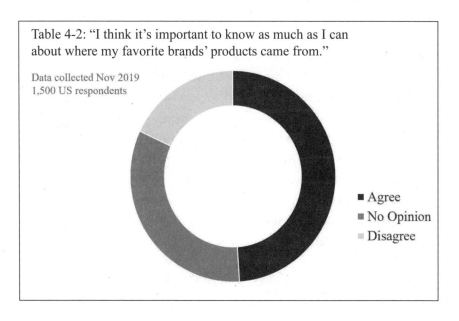

Table 4-2: "I think it's important to know as much as I can about where my favorite brands' products came from."

Data collected Nov 2019
1,500 US respondents

■ Agree
■ No Opinion
■ Disagree

it—suggests that the NBA is far more interested in embracing the inescapable presence of the smartphone and finding ways to connect the game plus technology experiences so that the NBA benefits, rather than trying to fight it. As Silver explains it, "How do we get them to engage in something directly related to that arena experience or what's happening on the court as opposed to looking at their friend's vacation pictures?"[4]

WHAT DOES THE DATA TELL US?

Consumer sentiment backs up this trend toward context and immediacy.

When we ask about trust in brands that seem to spend a lot of money on "marketing," we see 36 percent of US respondents saying they feel they're being lied to, versus 21 percent saying they aren't concerned. From our perspective, this isn't so much a question of whether the "yes" votes here fall short of a majority but rather that more than a third of all respondents agreed in the first place. This is a fairly damning indictment of how marketing is perceived in the marketplace. This basic measure of trust bears watching.

When it comes to context and background itself as a topic, 49 percent of US respondents—and 56 percent of US Millennials—believe it's important to know as much as possible about the brands they buy, including brand history and sourcing, where applicable. We want to understand the backstory.

In general, we're interested in context and love the sense of immediacy that this intersection of technology and culture has brought to the public discourse.

KEY TAKEAWAYS

Given what we've learned, how do we put these lessons to use? Here are the key takeaways and somewhat rhetorical questions we have to consider to get the most out of these insights.

How can we create more experts?

This is possibly one of the most important questions to ask ourselves as marketers: How can we create experts in our product category so that they will correct the wayward and evangelize of their own volition? What are the triggers that suggest a customer or a prospect wants to take that first voluntary step toward becoming an insider? What forums can be created—online or in-person—to transfer this knowledge? Who would do the teaching? How would we organize this group once they're trained? How would we ensure they know that we consider them experts, not just after the training but also every week and every month afterward? What's in it for them? And how can we use them as a competitive weapon against our competition in the field? All this is worth thinking through.

How can we educate instead of sell?

Our natural inclination as marketers—and as businesspeople in modern society, frankly—is to lapse into selling mode. As a result, it's counterintuitive to suggest that we stop and try something else. Do it anyway. How can we teach our prospects what they need to know in order to be expert customers? How can we shift from being marketers and sellers to educators, to publishers of educational material, so that we begin to add counterweight to the argument that all marketing is bad?

What are the cultural conversations—stated or unstated—in the market that aren't addressed?

Every business has sacred cows, elephants in the room, and other metaphors that describe the big questions left unanswered in the business. Some are consciously ignored on purpose by senior management because of fear that addressing them may upset the status quo. Some are known to everyone at the working level and strangely not at the senior level. We need to surface these and show them for what they are—in as raw and context-rich a fashion as possible. What is the truth behind digital security in your business? What's the truth behind performance characteristics and claims? What about sanitation and freshness, or transportation, or health impacts, or factory conditions? This is where raw context matters.

How can we show the actual evidence—the raw truth—to our customers and prospects?

We've explored a number of examples in this chapter that focus on raw video, or access to information, or apps—but let's not limit ourselves to these when we address this bigger idea of presenting evidence. Can we show the raw data and teach our audience how to interpret it? Can we show real-time monitoring of conditions, digitally captured and wirelessly transmitted? What raw evidence can we provide that removes any chance of doubt or any appearance that we're hiding something, even to the most cynical audience?

How can we take on the role of curator?

What happens if we hand the responsibility of content creation to our users? One would assume the natural home for this would be in the social world. But what if we reenter the conversation here and act as curators, not only of our own branded content but also of the content uploaded by the masses? Can we index and organize it so that it remains accessible? Can we simply do a better job of ensuring great content stays available for new customers when they come on board?

How can we vividly show our consumers the provenance of our product or solution?

If we believe that the origins of our products are important to discuss with our customers, how can we show them in a more vivid fashion where they came from? Are your ear cushions hand-sewn? Are your chickens raised on a small farm just outside St. Cloud, Minnesota?

Is your acoustic lab the most precise in the world? Is your theater the quietest on Earth?

Don't just tell me. Find a way to show me in as vivid a manner as possible. Because trust is running low and talk is cheap.

CONCLUSION

Marketing has become a bad word for a number of reasons, some well earned. The hard sell, the slippery nature of much of what we see on a daily basis, the always-on, act-now nature of the lowest quartile of marketing has unfortunately cast us all as snake oil promoters to some degree.

Against a backdrop of distrust, how do we win over a jaded audience? Many of us choose to entertain, hoping to earn our place in the cultural conversation by creating sticky, funny content that our best fans will share with their friends, even if the relationship between what's funny and what we do isn't always clear. Many are content to be purely transactional, focusing on those moments when the customer is ready to buy and ensuring they're available when the moment arises. Others focus on education, going beyond casual definitions of fandom and instead creating an army of experts who can't help but talk to their friends about what they've learned, because they've come to love the subject and need to share it. When we reflect on the nature of raw as a persuasive means of communicating, it's this last point—our ability to educate by providing a backdrop of relevant information that helps the viewer understand what they're seeing at a deeper level—that matters most.

Good marketers add context to the buying decision. They create empathy, a shared sense of raw experience that makes the viewer "one of us" and no longer an outsider judging us from a distance. Without closing this gap and allowing the audience to pass through this barrier to become one of us, our distracted audience, overwhelmed by the digital information overload that threatens to swallow them whole, will not know what to make of our message. It will get lost in the noise and the clutter. It will be ignored.

We've gone from a time of extreme intellectual curiosity and creation, driven by a hunger for scarce information, to one of extreme intellectual laziness, brought on by a super-abundance of information without the necessary context to allow us to make sense of it all. We have to work to bring our audience closer and help them connect the dots.

CHAPTER 5

Rule #5: Heroic Credibility

It's good—we gained about 20,000 followers in the last few days. Sales have gone up significantly. What people like is we are standing up for our brand.[1]

Arjun Seth, CEO of Protein World

In April 2015, a small British fitness and health supplement brand launched a minor ad campaign for its line of weight-loss products featuring a young lady in a bikini with the headline, "Are You Beach Body Ready?" causing 45,000 outraged body-shaming activists to sign a petition to have the ad banned, while another 400 or so protesters took to Hyde Park for a "Take Back the Beach" sign of solidarity.

Against this backlash, CEO Arjun Seth and then marketing chief Richard Staveley held firm, calling the protesters "feminist terrorists" and maintaining that their aspirational advertising shamed no one. More to the point, while the controversy swirled in the local press, the brand picked up an additional 30,000 new customers and saw an uptick of £2 million in sales, proving that you don't have to appeal to everyone to find those who respond to your message.[2]

Heroic credibility speaks to the willingness of brands and leaders to make bold statements that clearly, unmistakably, lay out their philosophy and values and then, in the face of criticism from the inevitable social-media-fueled wolfpack, refuse to back down.

There's more to heroic credibility than incendiary comments, however. As a matter of fact, this is a remarkably nuanced rule that requires careful thought and even more careful execution. Heroic credibility hinges on taking one of two potential directions: ownable brand values alignment (the smart direction) and brand militancy (the often-egotistical-and-leading-to-trouble direction).

Ownable brand values alignment speaks to DNA-level beliefs that are embodied through the brand. Nothing is bolted on. Everything is a self-defining statement.

With brand militancy, on the other hand, brands take polarizing social or political stances on issues that frankly have nothing to do with their brand, product category, or history, choosing to hector the market with lessons better left to other, more credible spokespeople. The DICK's Sporting Goods decision to remove all AR platform rifles from stores in February 2018 because the CEO wanted to make a statement after the Parkland school shooting caused the brand to lose $150 million, as the hunting and shooting community took their wallets elsewhere. One year later, the company was still feeling the impact (sales down $154 million and revenue down $51 million).[3] Gillette's "toxic masculinity" campaign in January 2019 resulted in a 2:1 negative reaction on YouTube and an avalanche of negative commentary on social media, causing the brand to pull its ad from the Super Bowl and, in the opinion of some analysts, caused Gillette's grooming product revenue to decline 1 percent in the subsequent quarter.[4]

Gillette and its lead advertising agency, Grey, created the "toxic masculinity" campaign because, as Gary Coombe, CEO of Global Grooming at Procter & Gamble, explained: "The challenge we have on the brand is to reconnect with the Millennial and Gen Z generations. . . . We know this group of consumers expects brands to stand for more than the delivery of their functional benefit. They expect these brands to have a point-of-view."[5] But the strategy backfired because Gillette and Grey did it for all the wrong reasons. "Toxic masculinity" was a bolted-on strategy, and consumers saw through it. The negative reaction on YouTube was still strong nine months later, with the negatives outweighing the positives by an almost 2-to-1 margin (1.5 million negative versus 802,000 positive).[6]

The message here is clear. Your brand actions must be in alignment with your brand purpose and values. If they are, tell the world what you are doing . . . and why. The world will listen, and you will be rewarded with loyal customers and brand advocates. However, if your goal is to increase sales by aligning with social issues that are not directly connected to your brand values, you will be punished by the marketplace.

THE PATH TO HEROIC CREDIBILITY

What if you are a brand, like DICK's Sporting Goods or Gillette, that sees a problem in society and wants to address it? Is there anything such brands can credibly do? Is it possible for companies to take a larger role in solving the nation's problems while at the same time making a profit for shareholders? Is corporate social responsibility ever credible if it is not part of a brand's DNA?

Answering those questions brings us into a larger conversation currently taking place in American business: what is the proper role of business?

"There is one and only one social responsibility of business," said economist Milton Friedman of the University of Chicago in 1970, and that is to "engage in activities designed to increase its profits."[7] Of course, Friedman observed, companies must obey the law, but beyond that, their only job is to make money for their shareholders. Friedman's view became known as "shareholder primacy," and it became the prevailing wisdom. In 1997, the Business Roundtable (BRT), an association of CEOs of more than 200 of America's leading companies, reaffirmed shareholder primacy in its statement of corporate purpose: "The paramount duty of management and of boards of directors is to the corporation's stockholders."

Then, in 2019, in a dramatic and historic shift, the Business Roundtable published a new statement of corporate purpose with five pillars: (1) delivering value to our customers; (2) investing in our employees; (3) dealing fairly and ethically with our suppliers; (4) supporting the communities in which we work; and (5) generating long-term value for shareholders, who provide the capital that allows companies to invest, grow, and innovate.[8]

Instead of just focusing on shareholder value, the new statement broadened the objective of the corporation to include four other stakeholders—its customers, employees, suppliers, and communities. JPMorgan Chase CEO Jamie Dimon, chair of the Business Roundtable, said: "[The new statement] is an acknowledgment that business can do more to help the average American. . . . The American dream is alive but fraying. Major employers are investing in their workers and communities because they know it is the only way to be successful over the long term."[9]

The business community and the business press did not take long to react. The *Wall Street Journal*'s editorial reaction: "[A] close reading shows there's less substance here than meets the media spin, but it's still notable that the CEOs for America's biggest companies feel the need to distance themselves from their owners. . . . Shareholders ride the caboose in this new code of corporate purpose."[10] The *New York Times* opined: "[The Business Roundtable's updated statement] was an explicit rebuke of the notion that the role of the corporation is to maximize profits at all costs . . . "[11] And *Fortune* and the *Economist* dedicated covers to the new statement.

Alan Murray, president and CEO of *Fortune* magazine, said: "I've covered business as a journalist for four decades . . . [and] in the past few years, it has become clear to me that something fundamental and profound has changed in the way [CEOs] approach their jobs."[12] And Murray had data to back up his perspective. In a poll conducted for *Fortune* in March 2019, 41 percent of *Fortune* 500 CEOs agreed with this statement: "solving social problems should be 'part of [our] core business strategy.' Only 7 percent agreed with the Friedman concept of shareholder primacy."[13]

The editors of the *Economist* wrote: "However well-meaning, this new form of collective capitalism will end up doing more harm than good. It risks entrenching a class of unaccountable CEOs who lack legitimacy. And it is a threat to long-term prosperity, which is the basic condition for capitalism to succeed."[14] In the *Economist*'s view, more competition, more innovation, and more diverse ownership are the keys to success, not a shift from shareholders to stakeholders.

Different commentators hold different views about what triggered the changes the BRT made to its purpose statement. However, there is widespread agreement that, among other problems, growing economic inequality, climate change, a health-care crisis, and a lack of effective governmental action are pushing companies to rethink their role in society.

Further, the public attitude about the proper role of business is changing. A July 2019 survey for *Fortune* discovered that 72 percent of Americans agree that public companies should be "mission driven" as well as focused on customers and shareholders. In that same survey, 64 percent thought that the "primary purpose" of a company should be to "make the world better," while the same percentage, 64 percent, thought the primary purpose of a company should be to "make money for shareholders."[15] The public hasn't rejected outright the concept of shareholder primacy, but it has begun to believe that companies need to do more. Americans want to do business with companies that care about both purpose *and* profit.

The concept of heroic credibility begins with the belief that companies should have a greater purpose than just making money. Business should be a force for good as well. If you are starting a company or if you are in the process of reinventing your company, we would advise you to begin by articulating your reason for being—beyond making money. What does your brand stand for? Why are you in business, and what are the values that will drive your business forward? Taking the time to get it right is worthwhile because everything you do, from that day forward, will be a function of how well you articulated—and then communicated—what you stand for.

VALUES-DRIVEN BRANDS

There has been a good deal of discussion lately about the importance of "brand purpose." Brand purpose, as expressed in the marketing literature, is a higher order reason for a brand to exist than just making a profit. Simon Sinek, the top evangelist for brand purpose, has a succinct definition: "People don't buy what you do. They buy why you do it."[16] The idea is that brand loyalty and brand commitment are driven by more than good products at good prices. People are drawn to you and your products or services because of *why* you exist. Sinek calls this "brand purpose."

We agree with Sinek that people don't buy what you do; they buy why you do it. However, instead of starting with purpose, we suggest starting with values. People don't buy what you *do*; they buy what you *value*. Companies with heroic credibility are driven by values—in many cases, DNA-level values.

For example: "We stand for equality. We stand for diversity. We stand for sustainability." Social responsibility values are important, but your values can also be product- or process-related: "We stand for quality. We stand for transparency. We stand for integrity. We stand for continuous innovation. We stand for maximizing long-term value."

Clear and well-articulated values will help you in everything you do: product development, supply chain management, customer service, marketing, and sales. Clear and well-articulated values will help you make decisions about what to do, who to hire, and when to change strategic direction. They will help you grow your business, and you will never be in a position where you need to back down (because of outside pressure). Your decisions will be rooted in your values.

BRAND VALUES ALIGNMENT

We believe in the concept of "values-driven" businesses more than "purpose-driven" businesses because they provide better guidance and more clarity for everyone—employees, vendors, and customers (and if you are a public company, investors). A set of core values acts like guiding principles that can be understood and followed by everyone.

Consider Coca-Cola's brand purpose (*coca-colacompany.com*): "To refresh the world. . . . To inspire moments of optimism and happiness." Or Zappos (*zappos.com*): "To delight people with experiences of joy, wonder, and limitless possibility." Or Starbucks (*starbucks.com*): "To inspire and nurture the human spirit—one person, one cup and one neighborhood at a time." All inspirational to be sure and causes to believe in. However, as a guide for management and staff to follow and as tools to build a strategy around, these statements are too lofty and too general. What you stand for and what you believe in must be more grounded. The problem with "purpose-driven" is that it is too grandiose, too difficult to operationalize, and too difficult to measure. Of what value is it to tell an employee "to inspire moments of optimism and happiness"?

A "values-driven" business, on the other hand, is easily understood and easy to operationalize. Your core values help you decide on Philip Kotler's famous four *P*s: Product: what you make; Price: how much you sell it for; Place: where you can buy it; and Promotion: how you promote it. Values help drive product, price, place, and promotion decisions.

MEASURING VALUES-DRIVEN BRANDS

Levi Strauss & Co. was founded in 1853 in San Francisco. Today, Levi Strauss & Co. is one of the world's largest branded apparel makers with more than 14,400 employees worldwide and $5.6 billion in revenue.[17]

From the very beginning, Levi Strauss & Co. was more than just an apparel maker. It was always concerned about the welfare of its employees and the people in the communities where the company did business. Click on the "Who We Are" tab of the landing page of the Levi Strauss & Co. website and you will find, in big, bold letters: "We are fueled by our strong values, creativity and hard work." Further down the page there is a message from Chip Bergh, Levi Strauss & Co.'s president and CEO. Bergh's message reads, in part: "Ask any employee what makes this company different, and they'll tell you. It's our values: Empathy, originality, integrity and courage. These guide every decision we make and every action we take. [Levi's is committed to] drive profits through principles."[18]

Profits through principles. Levi Strauss & Co. has always been guided by its principles approach to business and by its bedrock values. Over thirty years ago, one of the two authors of this book, Paul Leinberger, was a corporate manager in the Community Affairs Department of Levi Strauss & Co. "I can attest to the fact that Levi's was a different kind of place to work. All of us were proud to go to work there because we knew it was more than just a job. It may sound strange, because our business was making jeans, but that is not how any of us felt about it. We were making jeans, but we were also making a difference in this world. When you would tell someone that you worked at LS&Co, as we called it, they would always be impressed, because they understood that the company was more than just an apparel manufacturer. It made us feel good. To this very day, when I talk about working at Levi Strauss & Co., I still say 'we' when referring to the company. I have held many jobs since that time, but none of them has meant more to me." It is no accident that Levi Strauss & Co. has a far better retention rate than other companies in this business.

Levi Strauss & Co.'s values are easily understood and measurable. In terms of profits: "We are committed to reinvesting a portion of our annual earnings back into our communities." In terms of people: "We have a legacy of standing up for the causes we care about and empower our people to do the same." And in terms of product: "Our product donations support the needs of communities around the world in times of change."[19]

How does the company reinvest a portion of its profits? "We make an outsized impact by taking bold stands on social issues that align with our values of empathy, courage, integrity, and originality." Levi Strauss & Co. does not shy away from possibly controversial social issues, but it is guided by its values. Currently that means the company is involved in voting rights and engagement: "We are actively involved in efforts to *increase voter engagement* . . . [and] we give employees *paid time off* to vote and connect them with voter engagement volunteer opportunities" (underlining in the original). The company is also involved in gun violence prevention: "LS&Co. has pledged ongoing support for *gun violence prevention* by rallying the business community and advocating for gun safety measures" (underlining in the original).[20] As Levi Strauss & Co. demonstrates, heroic credibility is about living by a set of values.

BRANDS WITH HEROIC CREDIBILITY ATTRACT THE BEST TALENT

Besides attracting and retaining committed customers, a strong values-driven business also attracts the best talent. In 2018, Mercer, the world's largest human resources consulting firm, conducted a global study seeking to understand what employees *really* want from a company. What attracts them, and what does it take to keep them? Mercer identified three factors that both job candidates and employees want from a company. All three were somewhat surprising, given that many if not most companies do not focus on them or consider them as important factors. The first was job flexibility, with 51 percent of respondents wishing their company offered more flexible work options. The second was a commitment to health and well-being. According to this study, 50 percent wanted their companies to truly care about their physical, psychological, and financial well-being—not just subsidize a gym membership. But perhaps the most surprising and the most "underrated desire of modern-day employees is the desire to work with a purpose."[21] As explained by *Forbes*, interpreting the Mercer study: "Many employees would be willing to give up fancy nap pods or office game rooms in exchange for fulfilling work."[22] Mercer claims that "working with a sense of purpose boosts employee motivation, productivity, morale and overall job satisfaction." In fact, "thriving employees are three times more likely to work for a company with a strong sense of purpose."[23] Purpose, as used here, does not refer to a company's purpose as discussed earlier, but rather to an employee's understanding of the larger values espoused by—and lived by—the company. They are the tangible, measurable, actionable values that every employee can work toward every day and can see in action throughout the year. In that sense, a company's "purpose" and an employee's "purpose" are different. One is an aspirational and probably unattainable ideal ("to deliver happiness"), whereas the other is concrete and affirming.

A 2018 survey by Harvard Business School and Boston Consulting Group (BCG) on the future of work came to a similar conclusion. In this study, 43 percent of respondents said that what they wanted most from their jobs was "more interesting, more meaningful work"—second only to "better wages" at 45 percent.[24] And as was true in the Mercer study, Harvard Business School and BCG found that most business leaders were either not aware of or not yet ready to address their employees' desire for "more interesting, more meaningful work." Values-based work is increasingly among the most important drivers in attracting and retaining the best talent.

Pressure is also coming from young people and younger employees. According to the 2018 Deloitte Millennial survey, two items tied at the top of the Millennials' wish list of what they wanted from their employer or their prospective employer: "better financial rewards and benefits" and employers who are "proactive about making a positive impact on society."[25] The same poll, in the following year, found that not only did younger employees want to work for companies willing to take on social issues, but they were also favorably inclined to buy from such companies, while punishing those that were in business only to make a profit. In the 2019 survey, "42 percent have started or deepened business relationships because they believe companies' products or services are having positive impacts on society and/or the environment, while 38 percent have ended or lessened relationships with companies perceived to have a negative impact."[26] That's heroic credibility at work and in the marketplace.

BECOMING A VALUES-DRIVEN BRAND

What are the steps necessary to becoming a values-driven brand if you did not begin that way?

The Business Roundtable's new stakeholders definition of the purpose of a business (referenced earlier) is a good place to start. The 181 companies that signed the BRT's new purpose statement say they are committed to living by those values.

You can follow the lead of the BRT, or you can commit to becoming a "values-driven" company with your own set of values. If you choose the second path, what steps should you take?

The first step, in line with the BRT's fifth commitment (to generate long-term value for shareholders), is to shift your focus from the short term to the long view. Making this shift may be the biggest problem facing public companies, but it is also a problem for all companies. As Andrew Winston of Harvard Business School explains: "If you manage for long-term value, of course you need to account for customers, employees, communities and more. When we define value as this quarter's profits, we don't invest (and we certainly don't prioritize long emergencies like climate change). I believe that the current economic model incentivizes the liquidation of natural capital for profit."[27] So committing to long-term value is the first, and perhaps the most critical, step for companies to make.

It can be done. Back in 2009, Unilever CEO Paul Polman told the investment community that he was going to manage the company for the long term even if that meant giving up some quarterly profits along the way. He convinced many of the company's shareholders on his new strategy (and the others sold their stock). Since then, Unilever has done very well.[28]

Second, to become a "values-driven" company, you need to identify values that are authentic to you, that you can believe in *and* are believable to others (customers, vendors, shareholders, the general public). They must be connected to who you are and the products or services you provide. They must ring true. Both Gillette and DICK's Sporting Goods learned a hard lesson about the importance of authenticity.

Third, you must select values you, as a company, have a passion for. If they are not important to you and your employees, you will not be able to sustain them, and instead of working in your favor, they will become a deterrent and could possibly hurt your brand equity.

Fourth, you must commit to your values for the long term. Levi Strauss & Co. has lived by its values since its founding in 1853. That means you need to commit to values that are *not* driven by the latest crisis or your latest passion. For example, if you believe you need to be good stewards of the natural resources you use, commit to the larger value of "sustainability" instead of "recycling." At Levi Strauss & Co. "sustainability is literally woven into everything we do. It is how we do business and how we show up in the world."[29]

Fifth, choose values that can be measured. Ask yourself: how are we going to prove to our employees, our vendors, our customers, and to the general public that we are living by our values? If your value is "quality," what measures are you putting in place to demonstrate that quality is important to you? Can you see it in the materials you use, the vendors you choose to do business with, the retailers that carry your products? And since they can be measured, make sure you report on them—in your quarterly newsletters, in your reports to shareholders, in your company town hall meetings, etc.

Sixth, keep the number of values you choose to seven or fewer. Make the number manageable enough that everyone can remember them. For example, Levi Strauss & Co. has four, Nike has four, and Patagonia has four.

Seventh, keep the descriptions of each of your values as succinct as possible. For example, one of Nike's core values is innovation. Nike's description of innovation (*purpose.nike.com/innovating*): "To make big leaps, we take big risks." Easy to understand and easy to remember.

Eighth, connect your values to the performance objectives of everyone in the company. Reward adherence to the values and support employees who develop ways to strengthen your values.

One other important point to keep in mind: consumers now expect brands to align with their values, not the other way around. Brands that lose sight of this and believe that they are in the business of changing how society thinks about a subject on which they have zero expertise or credibility in the eyes of the consumer stand to lose money and trust. Therefore, in the beginning of your process to develop your brand values, immerse yourself in the lives of your customers. Become better listeners and participants in their lives. Learn what their needs and wants are; learn what is most important to them. Find out about their values and learn their vocabulary. And then do the same with your employees. Together, they will give you a strong base of understanding you can use to develop your own values.

WHAT DOES THE DATA TELL US?

When we look at our data, we see strong support for brands that stand for something bigger than themselves, with support across all demographics in the mid-50 percent range. This sentiment has been stable over the past four years of the study. When we asked for

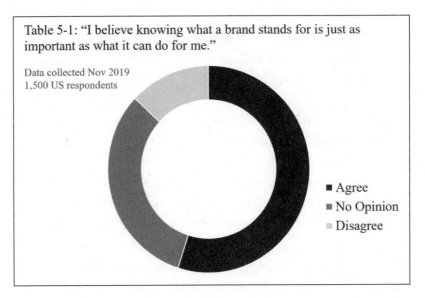

Table 5-1: "I believe knowing what a brand stands for is just as important as what it can do for me."

Data collected Nov 2019
1,500 US respondents

- Agree
- No Opinion
- Disagree

level of agreement with the statement "I believe that knowing what a brand stands for is just as important as what it can do for me," 55 percent of the total public strongly agreed or agreed with the statement, and that number rises to 58 percent with Millennials (ages 23–40 in 2019).

When asked whether a company's values are more important than taking a stance on social or political issues, there is overwhelming support for values. When we asked for level of agreement with the statement "I think that brands should focus on understanding their customers' values instead of taking the lead on promoting social and political issues," 77 percent of the total public strongly agreed or agreed with the statement, with Boomers rising to 82 percent.

KEY TAKEAWAYS

How do we start the process of becoming a values-driven company?
How often do we say, in other forums, to make sure we start with the consumer and not our own egos? The consumer now owns the brand relationship, not the other way around. We, as brand owners, are no

longer in charge and can no longer dictate the terms of the brand relationship. Knowing that, it is incumbent that you begin the process of developing your brand values by immersing yourself in the values, vocabulary, and lives of consumers.

What brand values can we own?

Heroic credibility is about the willingness of brands and leaders to commit to a set of values and then stand by them. To do this, you need to develop a mission statement and a set of values that are credible and believable. They are the DNA of your brand. They are your reason for being beyond making money.

The Levi Strauss values of "originality, integrity, empathy, and courage" act as guideposts for everything the company does. Originality drives its product development process. Integrity drives its sustainability policies. Empathy drives its employment practices and relationship with the communities where it does business. And courage drives the actions it takes on social issues.

Choose values that are authentic to you, that you can believe in and are believable to others. Make sure they are intrinsically connected to the products and services you offer. Select values you have a passion for. If your values are at the heart of who you are—deep in your DNA—they will guide your everyday actions as well as your strategy decisions. Commit to your values for the long term.

Ask yourself, what values should we own? What values will define who we are?

Do we want to do more than just make money for our shareholders?

The year 2019 marked the turning point for capitalism as we have always known it. When the Business Roundtable declared that the purpose of business should be to deliver value to customers, invest in employees, deal fairly and ethically with suppliers, support the communities where they did business, as well as generate long-term value for shareholders, it put the last nail in the coffin of shareholder primacy. The BRT validated the view that companies need to hold themselves to a higher purpose and need to demonstrate that commitment in everything they do. They need to embody it in their planning, their strategy, and their actions. The Business Roundtable validated the importance of heroic credibility. Now, make it one of your guiding principles.

How are we going to attract the best talent and keep them?

Companies like Levi Strauss & Co. are enduring proof that if you want to attract the best and the brightest and then keep them, be a values-driven company hallmarked by heroic credibility. In the past, such companies were the exception, not the rule. Today, however, if you want to attract the best talent, especially Millennials and Generation Z, you need to offer them more than a competitive wage; you need to offer them a job with a sense of purpose, a sense of meaning. The lesson here: to succeed and thrive in the second decade of the twenty-first century, make it clear to prospective employees that you are a company driven by your values and committed to heroic credibility.

How are we going to avoid the pitfalls of brand militancy?

Do not get involved in social or political causes that have nothing to do with your brand, product category, or history. Just because you have a board member who is passionate about something or a viral campaign is pushing you to take a stand on some social or political issue, don't do it. If you do, you may see a short-term gain, but in the long run you will lose the support of your customers, and revenues will suffer.

CONCLUSION

The concept of heroic credibility begins with the belief that companies need to do more than just meet the financial goals of their owners or shareholders. They have a responsibility to invest in their employees, deal ethically and fairly with their vendors, and support the communities where they do business (paraphrase of the Business Roundtable's new purpose of the corporation). Heroic credibility takes the concept of stakeholder responsibility one step further. Heroic credibility is about the willingness of brands and leaders to live by a set of values. Heroic credibility is about values-driven leadership.

PART 2

Synthesis

"What do we do now?" is a legitimate question after reviewing the primary macro trends we've just discussed. Once we've thought through how each impacts our businesses, we run the risk of not knowing exactly what to do with the insight we've just acquired.

Putting some of these insights to work is easy, thankfully. But when it comes to the real outputs of marketing—whether customer-facing or internally focused—we need to acknowledge that there are still a few more dots to connect.

We present two of these important connections here, in part 2, where we begin the process of synthesizing what we've learned so far into bigger concepts. We look at two big ideas in this part, starting with the shift to C2B and how these macro trends help us rehumanize the digital relationship, before continuing with a deeper look at how these trends impact storytelling in an age of digital distraction.

CHAPTER 6

The Shift to C2B: Rehumanizing the Digital Relationship

Millennials are the first generation in history to have the tools and the technology to be able to control their own worlds, including what they buy, who they engage with, what brands they choose to engage with, and all the rest. So, instead of being a B2C economy or a B2B economy, we are now a C2B economy. It is a dramatic shift in the balance of power.

Anne Bologna, former chief engagement
officer at iCrossing, in a personal interview
with the author on May 8, 2019

Raw, as a concept and as an operating principle guiding the way we now live our lives, is possible only because of the technology in our lives. And that technology, as Anne Bologna, one of the most brilliant advertising minds of the last quarter century, recognized: "We used to live in a B2C (business-to-consumer) world, where brands led and consumers followed. A world of captive audiences with limited choice. [Because of the technology available today] the business world is now C2B (consumer to business), meaning consumers lead and brands must follow." The polarity of how we do business has reversed. Companies and brands are no longer in charge, consumers are.

THE MOST IMPORTANT CHANGE SINCE
THE BEGINNING OF MARKETING

Since the end of World War II and the rise of consumer affluence (think the Populuxe era of the 1950s and early 1960s), consumer marketing has been defined by companies. Companies and their brands controlled marketing. We, as brand owners, marketed to "them" (consumers). We defined the terms of the relationship—what to buy, why to buy, when to buy, and where to buy. The entire advertising industry—from the 1950s to the turn of the aughts—was predicated on that dynamic. It was called B2C (business to consumer)— or B2B (business to business) if we were doing business with another business—and appropriately so. As brand owners, we dictated every aspect of the buying process. If you wanted to buy a new car, it was the car company that dictated the entire buying process: doing print ads and television ads (known as "awareness"); getting reviews of the new car in newspapers, magazines, and on TV and radio (known as "familiarity"); getting prospective buyers into showrooms (known as "consideration"); and finally getting the buyer to sign on the dotted line (known as "purchase"). And there was one more step, if you were lucky: getting the buyer to buy your car brand again (known as "loyalty"). In the car business and in other businesses, this narrowing process became known as the "purchase funnel," and entire industries grew up to support every stage of the funnel: advertising, marketing, consumer research, sales, fulfillment, customer satisfaction, customer retention, and customer loyalty. Other parts of the economy grew in support of every stage of the funnel: newspapers, magazines, television, radio, direct mail, and even retail.

Fast-forward to today. Newspapers are dying, magazines are going bankrupt, television is morphing into streaming services on multiple devices, and the retail landscape is looking bleaker and bleaker. There were 12,000 store closings in 2019, more than double the number in 2018 (5,854 stores), and estimates are that another 75,000 stores could be gone by 2026.[1]

Why is this happening? As we said in the introduction, technology has emerged as the single most profound cultural driver in the world today. We now live in a world where technology drives culture, and then culture shapes technology. Technology has reversed the polarity of the buying process—from a B2C world to a C2B world. Businesses are no longer in charge of the relationship. The consumer is in charge. Businesses can no longer dictate the terms of customer engagement; only the consumer can do that.

As Anne Bologna explains: "Consumers still want and need brands in their lives, but it must be on their terms. Customers want personalization, and they want brands that align with what they care about. Sixty percent of consumers do business with brands that share their values and beliefs, and 65 percent of consumers tune out brands that blast the same message over and over again."

The mainstreaming of personal technology and the explosion of consumer choice as the mobile internet came of age irrevocably and forever destroyed the traditional "purchase funnel," ushering in a new age of consumer empowerment. No longer do advertisers control the brand experience. When the screen moved from our television to our smartphones, and mobile internet access allowed us to search out product information (and pricing) even when we were in the very act of shopping—not to mention giving us the ability to provide a Yelp review, make a purchasing decision on Amazon with one click, or share an image of the product we were buying on Instagram—it became clear that the balance of power had swung away from brands and forever toward the now super-empowered consumer.

When brand engagement is viewed through the lens of the intersection of technology and culture, we now see a world where it has flattened, with activities once referred to as "top of the funnel"—like awareness and familiarity—now smashed down into the middle, and where "mid-funnel" processes—like consideration—are now instant requirements, even for first-time browsers.

This shift to C2B began about 2010 and accelerated with the widespread adoption of smartphones. In the early part of this century, two-thirds of all purchase decisions were driven by push vehicles— such as television ads. Then, as smartphone adoption grew, so did the use of pull vehicles—such as search, website content, and the like. The first year to see an over 50 percent share of smartphones in the United States was 2013 (51 percent in 2013; all cellphones—89 percent) and by 2019, the share of Americans who owned smart-phones had risen to 81 percent, with 96 percent ownership of any kind of cellphone.[2] And by 2019, over two-thirds of all purchase decisions were being driven by pull vehicles. Further, over half of all product searches were conducted on Amazon, not Google, validating the idea that we are firmly in the realm of purchase decisions—the bottom of the purchase funnel, not just casual interest. Consumers are now in charge of the purchase funnel, deciding to pick up their smartphones and initiate the search, rather than passively sitting on their couches absorbing brand-led advertising. This shift in the bal-ance of power has immense implications for brands.

"Fifteen years ago, when a client would come to me and tell me they wanted to grow their business, we would start the conversation around questions like: 'What does your brand stand for? What are your awareness numbers? What are your brand attributes?'" Bologna explains. "Now the conversation is: 'What's your digital presence? Is it optimized for search? Is it optimized for experience?' And we work up-wards from there. So, I think that is one of the biggest shifts. You start from the *bottom* of the funnel and work upwards. [However, that's not entirely accurate either], because there is no funnel anymore."

What happens when the traditional funnel disappears and the consumer has seized control of the brand experience? What exactly is a brand to do in this confusing new landscape? Increasingly, when consumers are now choosing to engage with you and your brand on their terms, the answer is deceptively simple: *be human*. "When an institution feels like an institution, my default is not to trust you," Bologna explains. "I want the brand to act more human, and that's no small thing, but it helps build trust and helps you engage."

In a C2B, "post-funnel" marketing landscape, where technology is the face of the brand and the interface with the culture at large, finding ways to rehumanize the digital relationship is critically important. The brand personality matters when it's the first point of contact with the organization.

A CONVERSATION, NOT A CAMPAIGN

How can we rehumanize the digital relationship? That is what chief marketing officers (CMOs), marketing chiefs, and business owners have told us is the single biggest challenge they face today.

They recognize that the marketing environment has swung dramatically toward digital in the last few years, and many have also recognized that their world has shifted from B2C to C2B.

How can companies address this challenge?

The blueprint begins to emerge when we combine the lessons of seeking control in an out-of-control world with raw in its many forms.

The first step is to simply recognize that you need to see the world as your customers do.

The lesson of seeking control is that your customers come to you believing that you can't be trusted. They no longer trust that companies have their best interests at heart. They no longer trust the institutions charged with safeguarding their personal and private information, and they no longer believe the sales and marketing messages of companies. In an environment where trust has collapsed, there is only one real and credible viewpoint your customers can trust: their own.

They trust their own eyes and ears—and their own responses. And they now have the technology in their pockets to do just that—take control of the process and do it their way.

The second step is to recall the elements of raw and then design to them. Operating in a state of rawness means removing ourselves as leaders or brand heroes and preferring to let the evidence speak for itself, allowing consumers to make up their own minds. Raw, as we have discussed, means unscripted, in-process, and in-context. What your customers want, and indeed now demand, is a buying process that is all of these things: information that is *unscripted*—"just give me the facts please, and in real time"; *in-process*—"give me the information I need to make a decision at this stage in my buying process"; and *in-context*—"understand my questions from my point of view, not yours. Answer my questions; don't give me the answers to the questions you have on your most frequently asked call-center script."

Therefore, start by ceding control to consumers and then, at each stage of the buying process, demonstrate that you are listening to them. Since they can start the process from anywhere, you must be ready to respond appropriately.

Let's look at an example to get a better idea of how this works:

You are looking for a pair of new shoes. While watching TV, you are also looking at your smartphone and monitoring another show on your tablet. You have three screens going at once, which is rather normal these days since most of us are spending over eleven hours per day on our digital devices.[3] You check your phone for messages and come across a Facebook post from a friend who has just come back from a shopping trip, and she uploaded a photo of her new shoes. You notice a link on the photo to the store's website, so you click that link. However, the doorbell rings and you don't go back to the store's website. Later, you pull up the store's website on your tablet. Recognizing you, the website shows the new shoes as a recently viewed item. The information also tells you that the shoes are in stock, come in five colors, and are on special right now. The information also tells you that the store is just ten minutes away—map included. The next day you stop by the store, and as soon as you walk in, your phone links to the store's Wi-Fi network, and the salesperson in the shoe department gets an alert that you have been reviewing that pair of shoes. The salesperson shows you the shoes, and you try them on. While you are trying them on, your phone checks prices at other stores and websites, downloads customer reviews, and provides you with additional information (where the shoes were made, who made them, and how they are constructed). You glance at the new information on your phone and then ask the salesperson about sizing and break-in time. Satisfied that the "special" price is indeed lower and because they are the quality you are looking for and because they look good on you, you buy them.

After a few days, the salesperson sends you a text asking how you like your new shoes. In fact, you like them so much you are considering buying another pair. You go back to the store's website only to discover that the special offer has expired. However, the site recognizes you (and the fact that you just bought a pair from the store) and offers you the special price. Gratified by the special treatment, you buy the shoes, which will be delivered the next day at the time you selected. A few months later, you receive a preferred customer invitation to an upcoming trunk show event at the store, where a personal stylist from the shoe company will be premiering next season's shoes (ahead of the announcement to the general public). You go to the show, and, again, the store's Wi-Fi system recognizes you, this time sending you a "welcome" text and a bar-coded coupon for use at the event. While you're at the show, the salesperson who sold you the first pair of shoes recognizes you and asks how you are enjoying both pairs of shoes (the salesperson knows about the second pair because the sale has been uploaded to your personal record; the salesperson also knows that you have accepted the invitation to the trunk show). The salesperson personally introduces you to the stylist, and you have your picture taken with her.

Here, the customer is in charge of the buying process, and there is no purchase funnel. At every stage of the buying process, the digital system recognizes what the customer needs and provides the information in real time. The process is highly personalized and, where appropriate, designed to simplify as many steps as possible. The system seeks to anticipate what the consumer might need and makes sure that the process is both integrated and ongoing. The process does not end with the sale but rather views it as the beginning of an ongoing relationship.

A seamless, streamlined, personalized customer experience. A digital experience designed to meet the needs of the customer at every stage of the buying process—a C2B experience, a rehumanized experience.

Such a customer experience may be rare today, but in the near future it will become commonplace. Increasingly, companies will shift their attention away from just selling products and instead focus on becoming experts in what Anne Bologna calls "human experience design."

HUMAN EXPERIENCE DESIGN

"Put simply, when you're designing an experience for your consumer, do you want it to feel like the DMV (Department of Motor Vehicles) or the Apple store?" explains Bologna, when asked to define the concept of "human experience design," or HXD. "Everyone knows the answer to that. The Apple store by all industry standards broke every rule in the book: how and where to merchandise, having a certain area for checkout, and putting certain items at the front. Because they built it as a brand experience, those rules don't apply, and yet it became one of the highest selling stores in all of retail. So it's a good example of not listening to conventional wisdom, and it's a human experience design that comes from a brand point of view. HXD is about doing the work, finding the insights, analyzing the data, and putting it all together so that a customer experience can feel completely intuitive."

HXD is about designing the digital experience from the customer's point of view. Customers experience the buying process as a journey, not as a funnel. Take the simple example of scheduling a doctor's appointment: you feel as though you might be getting the flu, and you have heard that available medications will lessen the impact of the flu if they are administered within forty-eight hours of symptoms starting. So you call your doctor only to get a long recording asking why you are calling and then asking you to tap a certain number on your phone that corresponds to the reason you are calling. You tap 4 because that's the option for making an appointment, and then you wait. You hear the phone ringing on the other end of the line, and after six rings, someone picks up and says: "Please hold." So you hold, while listening to insipid elevator music. After three minutes that feel like thirty minutes, someone comes on and says: "May I help you?" And you say: "Yes, I would like to see my doctor because I believe I am getting the flu." She says: "I'm sorry you are not feeling well. What are your symptoms?" You explain your symptoms to her, and she says: "Just a moment; I will have our scheduler get you an appointment." You are put back on hold and finally, after another three minutes, the scheduler comes on the line: "Can I help you?" "Yes," you say. "I need to see my doctor." She says: "Fine. Who is your doctor?" You tell her and then she says: "What time would you like to come in?" You give her a time, and she says: "I'm sorry, the soonest we could see you is on 'x' date, four days from now." You then explain to her why you need to see your doctor in the next forty-eight hours, and she says: "I'm sorry. The best I can do is put you on our wait list in case we have a last-minute cancellation." You say, "Thank you" but hang up ready to throw the phone against the wall.

What just happened? From the perspective of the staff in the doctor's office, they were all just doing their jobs and doing their jobs well. However, from the perspective of the patient, the experience was maddening—the exact opposite of what Bologna would call excellent human experience design. The employees in the doctor's office were working in their specific "silos," doing the job they were supposed to be doing. None of them could be faulted for their role in the call. However, from the patient's perspective, the call was a journey—and a rather rocky one at that.

The essential lesson here is to understand that when viewed from the customer's perspective (in this case, the patient), the process is a journey. The doctor's office has designed the process as a series of discrete steps with discrete outcomes (e.g., assess the patient's condition and then hand off to an appointment scheduler) that need to be followed in a specific order (i.e., first the assessment, then the appointment scheduler). The process meets the needs of the doctor's office but NOT the needs of the patient.

KEY ELEMENTS OF THE C2B EXPERIENCE

To rehumanize the digital relationship and shift the emphasis from "functional silos" to a customer's "journey," you will have to develop a new organizational structure (or dramatically revise the one you currently have), and you will need to develop a different cultural sensibility—namely, an obsession with your customer's experience. This will mean making customer experience a top priority across your entire business, from marketing to sales to customer service and product fulfillment.

Making this change may seem simple enough, and this advice probably sounds like common sense. How many times have you heard the call or said it yourself: be customer-centric. However, making changes to your organizational structure can be complicated, and, as any CEO who has ever experienced this will tell you, changing your organization's culture can be one of biggest challenges you have ever faced. We'll explore this issue in more depth later in this chapter.

To create rehumanized, world-class customer experiences, you will need to introduce several important elements into the redesign of your digital management system, starting with personalization.

Personalization has become table stakes. Consumers now live in an on-demand, multiple-device world that is ever changing, and they demand a level of personalization that has never existed before. Consumers have rapidly come to expect brands to understand how their individual needs are changing and what they are looking for now. Consumers don't want to be marketed to as part of a demographic; they want to be talked to as a market of one. Conversations, not campaigns. Consumers want an ongoing conversation with brands—one that they control, not a newly revised advertising campaign blitz. As Peter Kim, CEO of Mighty Hive, a digital advertising and marketing services firm, puts it: "It is crucial to move away from giant, costly campaigns once or twice a year to a constant conversation model."[4]

The next expectation is that you must be able to deliver this personalization in real time. "[Advertising agencies] need to create a human-centered brand experience that is more holistic," says Bologna. "It has to be powered in real-time to be relevant, engaging, and continuous, while meeting the various needs of the brand, the business, and the customer." You need to give customers the relevant information they need at every step in the buying process.

The next key step to focus on is simplification. "The goal should always be about taking extra work out of the process," explains Bologna. "Take extra steps out, add value, and radically simplify the process. . . . I like to think of it as an experience that delights and delivers, bringing value to the customer and producing results for the client. The essence, when applied to marketing, is navigating the consumer through a purchase funnel that is in sync with what they're doing versus what a business wants them to do." And be proactive.

If you know, from previous interactions with a customer or from existing sources, that certain kinds of information will be needed at this stage in the process, supply it without being asked (such as by providing price comparisons and reviews, as in the example).

And last, everything must be delivered for an omnichannel experience. Since consumers are using multiple devices to connect with your brand, your digital strategy must deliver an integrated experience from the customer's point of view. The newest data reports that 73 percent of all shoppers are using multiple physical and digital channels *before* making a purchase (compared with 20 percent in-store only and 7 percent online only).[5] Shoppers are looking for a seamless and consistent experience across every channel and device. Your messaging, objectives, and design need to be consistent across all devices, and every interaction needs to be seamlessly linked to every part of your digital brand system.

Your goal is to create an omnichannel experience that is seamless, convenient, and customer driven. When this experience is embedded throughout the customer journey and designed with the customer in mind, the payoff is significant. "A truly omnichannel operation that spans the customer lifecycle will optimize revenue, deliver capital efficiencies like cost savings, spawn operational efficiencies, and improve the customer experience overall."[6]

GETTING FROM HERE TO THERE: FROM TOUCHPOINTS TO JOURNEYS

Once you embrace the concept of C2B and acknowledge that the consumer is in charge of the brand experience, marketing investments shift from traditional advertising and promotions to consumer-centric processes. However, as Bologna explains, "The reality is we don't yet have systems in place to deal with the level of complexity and speed required to keep pace with consumers and innovation."

What challenges need to be addressed in order to develop a customer experience-based organization?

Since there was never a need for C2B companies in the past, none of the current organizational structures that companies use are adequate. You will probably have to change your organizational structure and your management system to become a true C2B firm. A landmark study by McKinsey in 2016 discovered that "[a]t the heart of the challenge [to deliver on the promise of a world-class customer experience] is the siloed nature of service delivery and the insular cultures, behaviors, processes, and policies that flourish inside the functional groups that companies rely on to design and deliver their services."[7] Most companies are organized as functional units, such as sales, marketing, customer service, and so on. As such, each department is measured and rewarded on its functional execution. The sales department is measured and rewarded for closing sales, not helping customers answer questions about the company's technology. In McKinsey's nomenclature, most companies are organized to deliver against "touchpoints"—"the individual transactions through which customers interact with parts of the business and its offerings." The customer service department can answer customer service questions, and the sales department can answer sales questions. But neither can answer questions that are out of their domain.

McKinsey's research revealed that companies could be delivering at all the touchpoints yet still be failing to meet customers' overall needs. A customer could be happy with the answers received from the sales department and the answers received from customer service and still come away from the overall experience very dissatisfied. McKinsey's advice is not only to focus on touchpoint execution but also to understand the "customer's end-to-end experience. Only by looking at the customer's experience through his or her eyes—along the entire journey taken—can you really begin to understand how to meaningfully improve performance." Every touchpoint silo (sales, customer service, technical support, etc.) might be functioning at a high level (as measured by the metrics of the functional units), and yet customer satisfaction could be low. To overcome the problem, McKinsey suggests taking a different approach: "Step back and identify the nature of the journeys customers take—from the customer's point of view" and "understand how customers navigate across the touchpoints as they move through the journey."[8] Focus on the whole, not the parts or even the sum of the parts.

Viewed from the perspective of the customers, every interaction with you has a context, and understanding the context is the key to understanding what your customers want and why they are navigating your system the way they are.

To be effective from your customers' point of view, you need to be able to identify where in the process the customers are and then provide the information they need at that stage—while at the same time understanding the context of customers' queries. Further, every stage in the process might trigger a feedback loop that takes the process right back to the beginning or jumps it forward to the very end. With the customers in control, the dynamics can get complicated fast.

This realization is a huge hurdle because how many companies want to rip up their organization chart and start over? How many companies want to introduce massive changes to their culture and reconfigure their managerial ranks?

Your first impulse will probably be to monkey around the edges, adjust the responsibilities of current managers, and make some minimal structural changes. From our perspective, that's a natural response. You may not want to make the changes necessary because you sense they will be too disruptive. And anyone who has ever spent much time in corporate America knows that organizational cultures are powerful and resistant to change. No one wants to abandon everything they have learned, and no one wants to see their job drastically changed or perhaps even eliminated.

That is why you have a major task ahead of you as you transition from a B2C culture to a C2B culture. New firms will have a head start because they can put together a C2B organizational structure and design C2B processes from the very beginning. No need for transitioning from one world to another. No need for disruptive organizational change.

It is too early to know what kind of organizational structure will work best. However, a number of companies across a range of categories (from hospitality companies to airlines to health-care companies) are experimenting with different designs and different kinds of managerial roles, and although no model organizational design has yet to emerge, some lessons have already been learned.[9]

CREATING A C2B CULTURE: A STEP-BY-STEP APPROACH

Experience to date from top-performing brands suggests that one of the most difficult aspects of this process is just getting up the courage to begin. Reorganizing around customer experience is a dramatic step; however, nothing will happen until you commit to it. Yes, you'll need a plan, but the first step is to announce your intention to begin the process and then figure out a place to begin. Find someone or some part of your organization where there is a desire to make the change. They can be your game changers.

Next, map your customer experience. Gather everything you know about your customers today. What is working and what isn't? Ask your customer service department what it knows (you'll be surprised at the wealth of valuable information the staff have). What are you hearing from your salesforce? Next, examine where the customers go to find out about you. How do you show up in search engine results? What is your social media presence? What brands are your customers cross-shopping? From here, map the customer journey in as much detail as possible with the cross-functional team best suited to add to this discussion. Don't leave anything out. Get the opinion of everyone on the team at each point in the journey and then document this information as best you can. This step means mining all your user data, scrutinizing consumer trends, and thinking through what the consumer decision process is. Then, once you have mapped it, go out and try it. Have everyone on the team go through the process in real life and then come back and see how well you did. And finally, identify places in the customer experience that seem to be broken (i.e., 65 percent of customers abandon their shopping cart at point of purchase).

From here, choose an organizational approach. While you have many different variants to choose from, your most fundamental decision is to begin by either changing how your functional teams operate or, more radically, to reorganize around cross-functional teams. Once you have made that decision, you can follow numerous road maps.

And finally, reorganize your staffing to support the customer experience. Bologna was one of the first senior executives in the advertising industry/digital marketing industry to pioneer a new C2B role. Her job as chief engagement officer was to oversee all of iCrossing's interactions with clients—and their clients' customers. She was responsible for the firm's "journey management system." In operational terms, that meant it was her job to oversee the "journey structures and processes" of all of the firm's clients. Reporting to her were a number of account managers (also called *journey product managers, experience managers, segment managers,* and *solution managers*) whose day-to-day responsibilities were to understand how customers move through the customer journeys, monitor each stage in every customer journey, suggest innovations based on feedback (such as customers leaving the site at a critical stage), constantly test and make improvements, and generally make sure that the customers' needs were being addressed in an efficient, timely manner. Assisting them were IT managers, operations specialists, customer service managers, consumer researchers, marketing managers, and others.

Journey-based management, as this new system is called, shifts attention to the needs of customers and away from a strict focus on selling products or services. In so doing, iCrossing has made the customer journey into a "product" itself. The company, and its clients, have learned that if you get the customer journey right and you continuously innovate and make it better, customer loyalty goes up, customer switching goes down, and the overall reputation of client companies goes up. iCrossing has changed its organizational design and its management structure to become more customer-centric, and its clients are winning in the marketplace with faster revenue growth and better customer satisfaction, and best of all, customers are getting a buying process that meets their needs on their terms. A rehumanized digital relationship.

WHAT DOES THE DATA TELL US?

When we look at the data, we see ample evidence that it is still early days in the digital revolution. The shift to C2B has only just begun. The data clearly shows that consumers are jaded by the disembodied digital persona that many brands have developed.

Most US respondents across all demographics say they get too many marketing messages in their inbox, with 63 percent agreeing or strongly agreeing. Further, consumers expect more from brands, with 55 percent of the general public agreeing or strongly agreeing with the statement "Brands should be able to know the nature of my problem and respond accordingly no matter which way I choose to contact them." As to the shift in the balance of power, nearly half (47 percent) say they've comparison shopped on their smartphone while in the act of shopping in a bricks-and-mortar store. This number jumps to 61 percent for Millennials. As for brand loyalty, a strong majority (65 percent) say they always comparison shop between brands when they want to buy something and 64 percent of respondents say they comparison shop between retailers. The data makes clear that there's a great deal of room for a rehumanized sense of customer care.

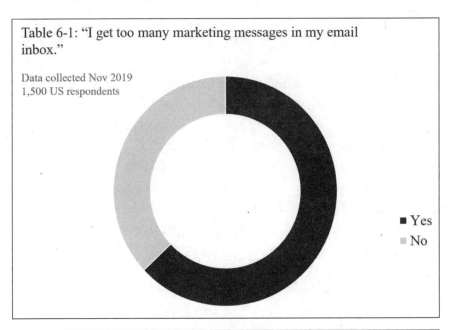

Table 6-1: "I get too many marketing messages in my email inbox."

Data collected Nov 2019
1,500 US respondents

■ Yes
■ No

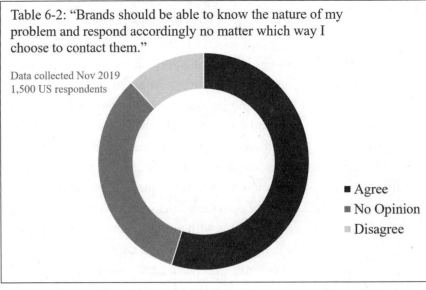

Table 6-2: "Brands should be able to know the nature of my problem and respond accordingly no matter which way I choose to contact them."

Data collected Nov 2019
1,500 US respondents

■ Agree
■ No Opinion
■ Disagree

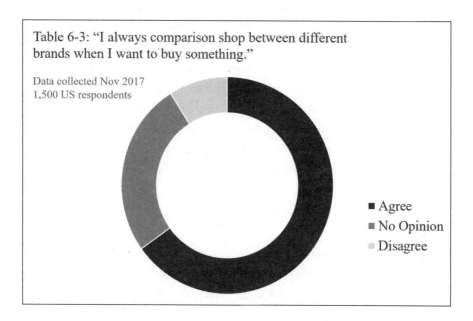

Table 6-3: "I always comparison shop between different brands when I want to buy something."

Data collected Nov 2017
1,500 US respondents

- Agree
- No Opinion
- Disagree

KEY TAKEAWAYS

Shifting your mindset from B2C to C2B is a dramatic, disorienting change, and doing everything that needs to be done will take time and patience. Let's look at the key questions to address.

How do we adjust to a C2B world?

In the most dramatic reversal in the history of marketing and advertising, what has always been a business-to-consumer (B2C) economy is now becoming a consumer-to-business (C2B) economy. Driven by the technology available to all consumers with a smartphone, brands are no longer in control of the purchasing process; consumers are. This means that you can no longer dictate the terms of customer engagement; only your customers can do that. "Customers still want and need brands in their lives," as Anne Bologna explains, "but it must be on their terms."

Since consumers have taken control of the purchase process, what must we do?

When your customers have seized control of the purchase process, what should you do? When the traditional purchase funnel has not only collapsed but disappeared, what should you do? The answer is deceptively simple: BE HUMAN. How can you rehumanize the digital brand experience? Begin by combining the lessons of seeking control in an out-of-control world with raw in its many forms.

How can we see the buying experience from our customers' point of view?

Recognize and acknowledge that in today's environment, trust has collapsed. Your customers no longer believe your brand communications. They are suspicious of your marketing and sales messages. To regain their trust, give them the information they need and let the evidence speak for itself.

Ask yourself: "How do our customers experience our buying process? What do they find easy? What do they find hard? Can they move from device to device effortlessly?" There are many, many questions to be answered. Your first step is to map the process.

Then, at every stage in their buying process, however they decide to move through it, demonstrate that you are listening to them by giving them relevant information (for that stage). Even better, if you know through experience (probably AI-generated) that certain kinds of information are usually asked for at that stage, be proactive and provide it without being asked.

To create world-class customer experiences, focus on three key elements of a C2B experience: personalization, real-time delivery, and consistent omnichannel experiences. Consumers now live in a multidevice, on-demand world, and they expect you to understand their (individual) needs. They are not part of a demographic; they are a market of one. Further, personalization needs to take place in real time, on their terms. And finally, make the process as simple as possible. Your goal should be to create a customer experience that "delights and delivers," as Anne Bologna likes to say.

To become a C2B culture, do we need to change our organizational structure?

Building an organization designed to deliver exceptional customer experience will require you to develop a new organizational structure or to significantly alter your current structure. You will make numerous changes as you evolve your system, but first you need to decide whether you want to modify your current organization structure or be bold and reorganize around cross-functional teams. After you have mapped your customer journey, turn your attention to this important task.

CONCLUSION

In a raw world, where consumers have taken control of the buying process, the goal of your business is to see the world from your customers' point of view. You need to shift your attention away from selling and instead focus on the customer experience. If you do, you will be rewarded with stronger revenue growth, more committed customers, strong brand equity, and most importantly, a rehumanized digital experience that meets the needs of your customers on their terms.

CHAPTER 7

The Flip Side of Raw: Storytelling in an Age of Distraction

It's not just that one brand story anymore, right? It's not just the TV ad that brands use to push out their message. It's become much more of a two-way dialogue. And that's the way I talk about storytelling today.

Nina Mishkin, former head of
global content strategy at Twitter, in an
interview with the author on September 20, 2019

If expectations have shifted to the point that technologically connected people the world over now prefer raw communication, what does this mean for traditional storytelling? You really can't throw a stone at any given social media feed without hitting a dozen heartfelt posts on storytelling for business. How does this hunger for a more immediate, unscripted form of communication play into the timeless nature of the conflict-and-resolution "Hero's Journey" process of storytelling?

Said another way, if we're all flocking to raw, does that mean storytelling is dead?

We don't see it that way, which should be good news to ad agency executives and brand marketers everywhere. We don't see the emergence of raw as a zero-sum game competing for funding with longer-form storytelling or advertising creative in general. We do think that raw deserves a place at the table, though, because it serves a complementary role in persuading our customers to believe.

Mishkin's quote reminds us that in this time of cultural techno-immersion, where the need to be the first to share stories with our network of friends is of paramount importance, we all want to influence the telling of the story. Customization and personalization matter to consumers, and they show up in our media habits. There's more to the story than just what the brand says. The brand can start the discussion, but fans on social media need to continue the conversation for it to exist in real terms.

But the impact of raw on how stories are told is more nuanced than just the number of characters used or the need for community involvement. We also need to think about the hunger for raw experience in the presentation of stories, showing us a side of life that would otherwise be hidden. We need to comprehend how technology is continuously providing us with more opportunities to deliver and consume this presentation of raw experience in a storytelling framing.

Advertising agencies have followed a fairly standard storytelling playbook since the 1950s that has served them well, for the most part. The marketing discipline is deeply invested in storytelling today, given the explosion of media choices that we have at our disposal. How brands can present their stories—and how agencies can tell them, both through creative and media—is big business. Figuring out how or when to use a raw approach—or just defining what a raw approach even means—is important.

Let's explore both vectors of this issue. We'll start with "long form versus short form," with the requisite discussion of the respective roles of the brand and the audiences it serves. We'll also look at raw from a creative point of view as well, discussing how technology allows us to present the perception of raw experience to the audience.

Between these two viewpoints, we'll build a better sense of how raw is used in the service of storytelling.

STORYTELLING IN 280 CHARACTERS AND THE ROLE OF THE AUDIENCE

When we look at the impact of technology on culture, one of the more profound outputs to shape how information is shared is social media. This is where we get our news, read the thoughts of people we have never met in real life but upon whose postings some of us have come to depend, and generally keep up a vibrant social life without ever saying a word out loud. Brands, as a result, have flocked to it. Spending on digital advertising of all types passed traditional advertising for the first time in 2019, and a sizable portion of this investment has gone to platforms like Facebook, Twitter, and others where interaction and commentary drive engagement. But regardless of relative shifts in total ad spending, is the story the same? Is the art of storytelling the same, regardless of whether you come across it as a television viewer sitting on your couch at home or scrolling through Twitter on your iPhone while you sit in mid-town traffic?

The answer, increasingly, is that it used to be the same . . . but now, it's not, and it's going to keep changing as we get better at it.

There's no better spokesperson for describing the growing specialization of storytelling on different media platforms than Nina Mishkin, former head of global content at Twitter. Nina's mission has been to evangelize to brands what makes this newer, faster, shorter medium important to brand strategy and how to take advantage of it.

"I get frustrated when I talk to brands, or creative agencies who think they should create digital ads with a TV mentality," Mishkin says. "They're using traditional storytelling arcs where the branding or the punch line comes at the end of the creative. If you're creating for a forced viewing environment, you can have as many tricks at the end as you want. If it's not a forced view environment, how are you going to capture and retain the consumers' attention? Consumption patterns have changed. Many environments aren't forced view; many platforms offer opportunities for the consumers to engage with the content and converse with the brand. As an advertiser, it's important to put yourself in the shoes of the consumer and create something that fits with the consumption process."

The first major macro trend we discussed was seeking control in an out-of-control world, describing how all of us in an environment awash in information are looking for ways to wrest some sense of control back in lives we feel are spinning out of our hands. This effort applies to media consumption as well. Unlike captive audience experiences, where viewers can't avoid ads (like movie theaters), social feeds move fast. As a result, users are in complete control of the experience, quickly scrolling past interruptions. This capability creates a real problem for storytellers hoping to get their messages in front of social consumers, particularly, as Mishkin says, when so many of these storytellers are stuck in a "television mindset." So how do we persuade our audience of viewers to stick with us? Or, conversely, do we build contingencies around them not sticking with us and cater instead to a much shorter attention span? This constraint may fly in the face of decades of advertising practice, but it's a constraint we're forced to face.

"You do really kind of have to throw out our old way of doing things," Mishkin says. "You have to capture attention quickly, and you have to deliver your key message very clearly in the first few seconds in order to make an impact. You need to think about how to creatively make your brand and product a prominent part of the creative. You need to think about designing for [a] sound-off environment. And you have to think about how you're going to hook people in those first few seconds so they stick around."

How should we look at storytelling now that the media landscape—and the attention span of the individual citizen on the street—has fragmented into so many different choices, each demanding a different sensibility?

THE HUMAN GAME OF STORYTELLING, ONE NEW SPIN AT A TIME

The best strategy in today's mobile-first, highly interactive world, as Mishkin describes it, is to think of brand narratives as a series of concentric circles. The story that the brand tells sits in the bull's-eye. "If you think about a series of concentric circles, that brand story, that brand's message, gets further disseminated outwards as brand ambassadors and consumers spread that message," Mishkin explains. "The next circle might be celebrity spokespeople. How do they take that message, interpret it, and put their own spin on it? The good brands make sure that their message stays true to the core story, while still feeling authentic to the voice of the ambassador. They're just asking somebody else to become the author."

"The next level might be influencers," Mishkin continues. "How are influencers adapting and interpreting a product or a brand story? Then, the next level is going to be consumers. Brands want to be something that consumers are talking about. They want to influence the conversation. To do this, brands must tell a story that consumers want to share and/or participate in. In this way, brands become part of the conversation and, thus, are more relevant to other consumers. Executing this strategy successfully allows for a brand's story to be amplified across social networks, capitalizing on the earned potential of an interactive feed. And when each of those concentric circles successfully track[s] back to the core message? To me, that's the Holy Grail for advertisers."

What's critically important here is defining the role that each player along this path is responsible for. Everything starts with the brand and flows outward, from authority and micro-authority figures toward the general consuming public. Everyone is expected to touch the story. If the story isn't touched, spun, or made personal, the story dies before it crosses that invisible barrier into "cultural narrative."

"The reality is, people believe recommendations and referrals and comments from their friends and family," Mishkin says. "So, the issue for brands is how to get others to start telling their story, because it's actually the power of the others that [is] going to have a much bigger impact. Whereas the most many brands can hope for is to just create a transactional relationship, if I'm a really great storyteller, maybe I can make somebody feel something."

It's likely that the roots of this step-by-step progression of storytelling lie somewhere between the twin psychological pillars of social proof and exclusivity. Social proof, on the one hand, suggests that we find something more persuasive when other people, similar to ourselves, take some sort of voluntary step toward supporting it. This step could be something as minor as a "like" on Facebook or something as major as a social media influencer writing a thoughtful comment while sharing or retweeting a branded statement. On the other hand, exclusivity suggests that things are perceived as being more valuable when they are scarce or time sensitive. This factor plays a role when we think of timing, specifically the aging of information on social media. The desire to lay claim to a story within the circle of contacts speaks to the basic desire of being seen as influential. But as we've seen in other studies, the shelf life of social media posts runs between a day or so to mere minutes. Being first matters in a game of speed, when bragging rights and public perception are on the line. And the more a brand can connect to timely events in the lives of its followers, the more culturally relevant and sticky that brand's message becomes.

We also see a clear desire on the part of the outer concentric rings—from the celebrity spokespeople to the influencers to the public—to add their own personal take on the story. We have to touch things and make them our own, particularly in this medium. The rise of narcissism as a societal trend, from the desire to customize our belongings to feeling that we're all entitled to comment on news articles we read online, points to the desire to take what is given and change it to suit the individual's personality and self-image.

Viewing these three forces together, we see the brand's stated desire: create a sense of momentum behind branded stories and narratives, where stakeholders in each concentric ring add their own personal spin on the story, as quickly as possible so that the story is perceived as not just fresh but also important to important people. Social proof plus exclusivity, with a dash of narcissism.

THE MEDIUM IS ALSO THE STORY

Another constraint we need to think through when defining how stories are best told against this technological backdrop is understanding which messages are best for which media. And this comes back to our ever-shrinking attention spans.

"I think what we're struggling with from a marketing perspective is telling the right stories in different places and then knitting everything together," Mishkin explains. "So, you're telling a consistent and cohesive brand story, pushing a consistent cohesive message, but being conscious of all the different places where that story will play. What does a message from a brand look like in a podcast? What does it look like in a mobile feed or a social feed? How do you think about longer-form content that could run in the right place, like a movie theater? We used to be able to think about the channel later. And now we really have to think about them much earlier and understand what the expectations of consumers are on those different platforms."

A good example of doing this right can be found in how the more forward-looking Hollywood studios promote their cinematic releases, from traditional trailers in the theaters and on television to the smart way many are using social media to tell nuanced stories-with-stories to different audiences. For the 2019 Disney release of *Dumbo*, different trailer concepts were launched for parents, kids, Millennials, and others, each with a slightly different style and hook. Where one focused on the flying elephant, another focused on the love story subplot, while a third played up nostalgia. Speaking about the film's promotional efforts leading up to its opening, Mishkin said, "The content that they ran in all of those placements perfectly complemented that specific environment and audience. *Dumbo* was everywhere, but you weren't seeing the same *Dumbo* ad in every place."

Other smart brands are taking a similar approach by identifying specific points along the customer journey and creating different content strategies for each key player along the way. Is the product made for men but bought primarily by the female head of household doing the shopping? Different audiences drive the need for different content strategies, and each requires its own creative treatment.

Storytelling on an interactive platform—in short form, served up to distracted viewers with their thumbs poised over the skip function—is a question of brands acting as fire starters. Their job is to strike a match. And if it ends there, the brand has failed. The point, therefore, is to ensure the discussion is picked up by the next circle of viewers who will add to the story and take it forward to their individual networks. And this has to happen quickly.

Otherwise, brands just find themselves repurposing television advertising for social standing alone on their respective digital soapboxes, competing with the deafening roar of other distractions.

When we think of raw as that collection of unscripted, in-process, and in-context communication streams, we can readily see how these different animations of the point fit in the preceding discussion. The brand is counting on the audience to add their thoughts, and in most all cases, these will be unscripted. Many will be thoughts or opinions in-process, soliciting further comments and inputs. Often, these retweets and shares will provide greater context to the discussion, adding personal stories and breathing more life into the brand's original intent.

In this sense, it isn't always the brand that has to be on the hook to produce raw content; sometimes, the intent is to solicit fans, evangelists, and influencers to do it for them. This isn't a huge ask, either. We all have video cameras and mobile internet in our pockets. We are walking video-production facilities, and none of us have the time or patience (almost none of us, in any case) to spend much time on production when the issue is current and we want to be the first on the block to share it.

How else can we animate this concept of raw when looking at storytelling? Let's turn our attention to the pursuit of raw experience and explore how filmmakers are breaking down traditional barriers—for both audiences and actors, themselves—in the pursuit of a more authentic, raw experience.

IN SEARCH OF RAW EXPERIENCE

The hunger for raw experience is clearly an emergent trend in this intersection of technology and culture, influencing everything from politics to business to sports, plus a number of other areas of cultural importance. And since we're on the subject of storytelling, we'd be remiss if we didn't discuss the actual art and science of filmmaking within this conversation. Whether the story and film are presented through heavy computer-generated special effects or just "two actors and a lightbulb," stories—particularly on film—give us the "equipment for living," to paraphrase literary theorist and poet Kenneth Burke. Given our more modern sensibilities, now shot through the prism of technology, this desire for the experience of life is heightened when we're able to bring the viewer closer to the real action.

How does this work, then? How can technology bring us closer to what the filmmaker intended?

One way is to remove all the equipment, eliminating the barrier between actor, director, and audience.

"When you're shooting on the iPhone, you're no longer a camera guy," independent filmmaker Tristan Pope said in an interview with the author on September 30, 2019. "Well, you're still the camera guy . . . but you're also the director. It's a different medium where you're behind the camera the whole time, right there with everybody else."

Pope's 2014 short film *Romance in NYC* was one of the earliest examples of what would ordinarily be a traditionally produced film but shot instead on an iPhone 6. The first-person perspective film shows, without dialogue, a day in the life of a couple in New York as seen through the eyes of the boyfriend. This short film written, shot, and produced by the Emmy-award winning filmmaker went on to win nine awards, including the New Media Film Festival's "Best Mobile" award in 2015, as well as garner a nomination for Best Film at the iPhone Film Festival.

Shooting with an iPhone is a different experience—both for actor as well as director. Usually, the director isn't right there with the actors in the scene. The director is slightly off the set, staring at a monitor. The detachment is part of the job when you're relying on a traditional camera rig, operated by a cameraman and overseen by a cinematographer. The director needs to view the emerging film through the eyes of the audience. But the dramatic improvements in picture quality that smartphones provide have changed the rules.

The physical equipment that was once an imposing physical barrier between actor and filmmaker is now gone, too. The psychological impact on the actor of "being on camera" is replaced by the everyday notion of performing while someone is recording them on a mobile phone. The physical distance between actor and camera can now be shrunk down to a matter of inches. Instead of facing equipment, the actor now faces . . . another person, who is literally so close and so intimate that capturing the action itself becomes an afterthought.

The result is immediate. "You get a more personal experience with the actors," Pope says. "There's literally nothing between you and them. It's just a little thin iPhone, right? When you're on a film set, you've got a giant rig, and you've got someone running that rig, and then you've got three people really focused for that rig, and then you're sitting in a chair behind that rig. The actor is very far away from you. But when you're on an iPhone, you're always right there with the actor. You're laughing and you're having a good time when you're shooting and you're creating a bond with these actors, more so than I think you would when you're doing it the other way around."

RAW EXPERIENCE AS A FUNCTION OF TECHNOLOGY AND FLOW STATES

Compare Pope's experience working with actors—without the heavy equipment interfering in what can be, on film, the performance of an emotional or sensitive scene—with the psychology of flow states, where capabilities and skill sets meet the challenge at hand, producing a state where we "lose time" in an activity. Technology is always most effective when it's invisible to the user. This goes for productivity devices, user interfaces, and apparently cinematic camera equipment, even when the equipment used is the humble smartphone. If a filmmaker can reduce the amount of physical equipment facing the actor when shooting a scene, this effort produces a less artificial environment. Even the most experienced actor would have to agree that there is a difference between performing in front of a full cinematic camera rig and another human being holding an iPhone. In Oscar-winner Steven Soderbergh's 2018 independent film *Unsane*, lead actress Juno Temple discussed this nuance, saying, "The iPhone created a greater intimacy . . . you would sometimes forget it was there. It could be put into places that would make the scenes up close and personal."[1] Soderbergh himself sums up the experience of filmmaking with a smartphone, saying, "I look at this as potentially one of the most liberating experiences that I've ever had as a filmmaker, and that I continue having."[2]

In a Hollywood age dominated by big budget, big CGI visual spectacles that satisfy a hunger for escapism, shooting cinematic movies with smartphones may well usher in an era of the true democratization of filmmaking. Once the capital requirements of making (or distributing) a film drop to levels that no longer require big production company backing, we will likely see the disruption of an entire movie-making system, not just in the United States but also globally. If the price of entry is a smartphone, a good screenplay, and a vision for the whole, why can't we expect a global explosion of talent and an expanding universe of good stories streaming on a device near you?

THE BOARD HAS HEARD EVERY LIE IMAGINABLE: STORYTELLING IN THE BOARDROOM

It's seductive to think that our world of storytelling and brand narratives is confined to impersonal, one-to-infinite audiences, but we'd be smart to remember that perhaps the most pressing of all applications is far more personal, intimate, and frightening. Storytelling to a small group of board members is often the most high-stakes narrative an executive can make. The good news is that everything we've discussed thus far still holds. The need for crafting the right creative, setting the timing of the hook, and selecting the right messages for the right audiences in the right moments is still of paramount importance.

The corporate storytelling-industrial complex has become a boom-town industry today, with pundits, authors, workshop gadflies, and others all fighting for scarce leadership development dollars earnestly deployed to help those in corporate life tell better stories. Why the interest in corporate storytelling? The reason is simple.

The board has heard every lie imaginable.

They'd just like to get to the truth. This isn't just a question of bad slides and poor presentation skills, either. It's more to do with risk aversion on the part of terrified executives.

When it comes to finding an authority to speak on the subject of storytelling, it's hard to find a more unarguable expert than Hollywood icon Robert McKee. McKee's students have collectively garnered 60 Academy Awards (and 200 nominations), 200 Emmy awards (and 1,000 nominations), 100 Writers Guild of America awards (and 250 nominations), and undoubtably created millions upon millions of PowerPoint presentations in boardrooms across the world.

"When you do a PowerPoint presentation, you hide everything negative behind your statistics and your quotes from authority," screenwriting teacher Robert McKee tells us. "When you tell a story, the whole gist is to admit the negative side, then dramatize the positive side of how the courageous little company overcame all the negatives."[3] The issue, more often than not, is to get executives to admit that they made a mistake. Getting them to admit, before their peers or management, that, for a split second, they were not omniscient and in control is terrifying. While that may be a frightening concept for an executive in the wrong sort of culture, it's both the heart of storytelling and the answer to the board's plea for honesty.

McKee's words resonate because we've all lived through them in our lives at work. Much of the communication that takes place in business is based on lies of omission and commission, as anyone who has ever sat through a sales pitch or a board meeting can attest. But it's important to focus on this point for a moment, because for many of us, our boards, management, peers, and subordinates all have access to much of the data we've used to construct our presentations. We have cloud-based financials. We have voice-enabled search and feed aggregators that can quickly summon data in the midst of a conversation that can either provide clarity or create greater confusion, depending on the context. We are awash in data. What we often lack is the ability to make sense of it all. What separates the data from the noise, and the agendas of everyone in the room from the desired outcome, is the ability to persuasively weave the data and insight into a cohesive story, one that takes us from where we were to where we are and points us to where we want to go.

But we're living in a time and age of not just ubiquitous information but also of skepticism. As we've already exhaustively discussed, we don't trust the institutions around us anymore. That includes our own companies and, at times, our own management. And if the board has heard every lie imaginable, then it's likely they won't simply sign off on whatever the PowerPoint deck says.

FROM PROTAGONIST TO GREEK CHORUS

This bigger idea of raw matters for exactly this reason. It helps persuade when trust may be less than rock solid. Avoiding the heroic nature of management as protagonist and shifting our perspective to instead embrace the role of Greek chorus, providing context instead of the hard sell, is how we work with a distrusting audience. It's not just disarming. It's genuinely, authentically credible. We can show our board members the evidence and teach them how to interpret it. We can discuss how we see it and how they, too, could interpret what they're seeing. But make no mistake, our job is still to tell a compelling story, explain what all this means, and chart the path forward. Raw lets us sidestep the harsh glare of the spotlight and offers us a seat at the audience's side, while we confidentially whisper in their ear and teach them how to interpret what we're showing them. By providing context and expertise, we can allow the audience to reach their own conclusions and trust not our rhetorical skills but their own judgment.

In this sense, our role as corporate storytellers is less about winning the argument than it is about teaching us all how to interpret complexity and then, in the midst of it all, navigate the way forward.

WHAT DOES THE DATA TELL US?

When we ask people about how stories impact their relationships with brands, we get interesting answers. It can be tricky to ask someone whether they respond to stories, just as it is difficult to get anyone under the fluorescent lights in a focus group room to admit that they're swayed by advertising. Most of us, if pressed, will find ways to defend our rational sides before we're even willing to acknowledge that we have an emotional one. We hate admitting we're persuaded by anything other than cold, impartial facts, usually carefully mined from our own research and subjected to the harsh glare of our judgment. Be that as it may, if we can use a bit of misdirection, sometimes we can get to the truth after all.

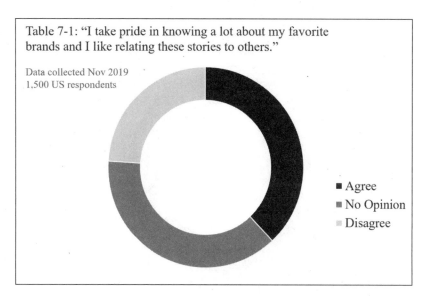

Table 7-1: "I take pride in knowing a lot about my favorite brands and I like relating these stories to others."

Data collected Nov 2019
1,500 US respondents

- Agree
- No Opinion
- Disagree

When we asked US respondents whether they take pride in knowing a lot about their favorite brands and—importantly—relating these stories to friends, we see some evidence that they do, with 38 percent agreeing and 24 percent disagreeing (the remainder stating no opinion). This number jumps to 47 percent agreement for Millennials, with only 19 percent disagreeing.

Further, we find a full 55 percent of US respondents agreeing that knowing what a brand stands for is just as important as knowing what it does for them, suggesting that there's more to brand mythos than just speeds and feeds. When we look at this data point against the backdrop of the preceding question about readiness to tell branded stories to our friends, it resonates. We like to feel good about the brands we buy, and we like to signal these feelings to others.

When we look to technology to help us understand stories, we get real generational splits, likely due to the general nature of technological familiarity. Technologies like body-worn cameras, livestreaming, drone videography, and augmented reality (AR) now allow us to virtually step into someone else's life experiences and see

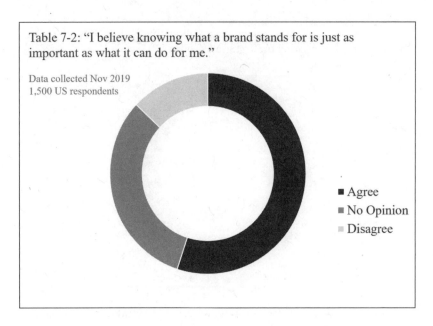

Table 7-2: "I believe knowing what a brand stands for is just as important as what it can do for me."

Data collected Nov 2019
1,500 US respondents

- Agree
- No Opinion
- Disagree

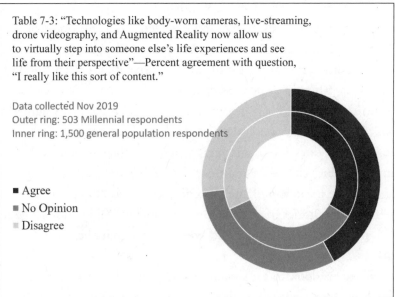

Table 7-3: "Technologies like body-worn cameras, live-streaming, drone videography, and Augmented Reality now allow us to virtually step into someone else's life experiences and see life from their perspective"—Percent agreement with question, "I really like this sort of content."

Data collected Nov 2019
Outer ring: 503 Millennial respondents
Inner ring: 1,500 general population respondents

- Agree
- No Opinion
- Disagree

life from their perspective, as Tristan Pope's *Romance in NYC* shows us. Asking whether respondents like seeing that sort of content, US respondents in the general population are split roughly into thirds between agreement, disagreement, and not having an opinion, but asking this same question of younger Millennial respondents reveals a significant shift, with 42 percent showing interest versus 27 percent uninterested. As familiarity with technology increases, we see a greater gravitation to explore what it can do for us and how it can help us see other sides of life.

Lastly, we can point to a statistically relevant data point that confirms for us that the Hero Myth is alive and well—a total of 54 percent of US respondents say they identify with underdogs and like it when the little guy wins.

What do these data points suggest? We have good evidence that US respondents like the idea that the brands they buy mean something more than just the bundle of their features: we identify with the key brands we buy. They help us create a self-image for ourselves. This image comes to life when we learn about the stories that make up the brand image and then pass these stories on to our network of friends, both online and in person. We still believe in underdogs, coming from obscurity or from positions where they arise from the canvas to fight again, and want to see the downtrodden win. This is as much a part of our Western culture as it is a continuing indictment of the lack of brand loyalty to which we've become accustomed. Living in this age of collapsing trust just compounds the issue.

KEY TAKEAWAYS

What is the brand's job in promoting its stories? And what do we expect of our customers?
The first big insight is that we can and should label and consciously address each concentric circle of our communications plan, piece by piece. As Mishkin describes the way she coaches brands to leverage

Twitter, the brand's job is to play the narrative role, producing top-quality content that is both sticky and sharable—from celebrities to influencers to the general public. We, as brands, need others to pick up the story, make it their own, and run with it. Otherwise, the story dies on the vine.

How does the timing of the hook play into our storytelling through different media?

Once we take into account the control we have—or don't have—over our presentation of a story, it changes every assumption we need to make regarding how the story unfolds. Is the audience captive in their seat, excitedly waiting for a movie to start? Or are they distractedly scrolling through a social feed, flicking their thumbs past anything that doesn't grab their attention quickly? What a difference, thinking about the mental and emotional state of each case! And when Mishkin talks about her frustration when dealing with agencies who are stuck in the thirty-second commercial mindset, it becomes clear that this distinction isn't widely understood. When designing for a viewing environment where the viewer controls whether they stay or leave, we need to set the hook early—closer to a Hollywood movie trailer than a prototypical Hero's Journey.

How do self-service technology platforms help us tell overlapping, nuanced stories?

Again, by shifting our point of view regarding where and how we're looking at stories, we see the big opportunity to tell multiple streams aimed at different people along the buyer's journey. If you're a fan of classic, iconic cinema, you've probably seen (or studied) Akira Kurosawa's film, *Rashomon*, telling the story of a murder from the widely differing perspectives of four people (one of whom is dead). How many ways can we borrow a page from Kurosawa and tell our story from multiple viewpoints, aimed at different people, playing different roles?

How many ways can we capture raw experience?
The great democratization of technology has put the means to capture human experience at our fingertips like never before. Director Steven Soderbergh has referenced an anecdote in recent interviews describing not liking the setup of a shot and finally taping an iPhone he's using to shoot the scene to the wall. Think of this as a metaphor, for the moment: how many ways can we employ the technology we have at our disposal to give our audiences a first-person point-of-view look at the experience we're presenting? The means to tell complex, emotional stories that satisfy this hunger for raw experience are exploding all around us. How can we make a conscious decision to use them to their best possible effects?

How does big, sweeping emotional narrative fit with raw, evidence-based rational data?
The interplay between long-form sweeping narrative and the shorter, more visceral, raw experience is how we win over skeptics and tell persuasive stories in this day and age, particularly when you're face to face. This nuanced toolset allows us, as storytellers, to play directly to the hunger for raw that we all have developed; in a time of collapsing trust, we only believe what our judgment tells us is reasonably true. We want the evidence—the raw feed, the data, the hidden video—and so it's our job, as storytellers, to provide this. But that doesn't mean we don't also play the role of narrator, setting the scene, teasing out the meaning and context of the data, and showing the audience where the story goes.

In this sense, the combination of long-form narrative and shorter-form raw communication—whether it be teaching the interpretation of data, showing the hand-held video recording of what's really happening in the street, or capturing the live reactions and emotions of new customers when they experience your product for the first time—serve to hit both the emotional as well as rational needs of the audience.

It's a beautiful yin-yang, left-right combination that appeals to a twenty-first century skeptic's hunger for truth.

CONCLUSION

After this exploration of the hunger for raw against the backdrop of storytelling, have we come out believing that stories are dead? We're guessing the answer is a firm "no." We've uncovered a far more nuanced view of the relationships between the two. This isn't so much a question of tension as it is the definition of a symbiotic relationship—between long- and short-form stories, of highly stylized and spontaneously developed content, of rational and emotional triggers presented in the flow of a story, and of the placement of the hook (or climax) at the beginning or end of the story itself.

Raw hasn't shouldered storytelling out of the way; it simply provides us with new formats, nuances, and opportunities to tell compelling narratives. It is, in its own way, storytelling itself—sometimes in a different medium, sometimes using different means of production to achieve a different effect on the audience, and sometimes acting as a persuasive device so that others can see the reality of a situation without the benefit of first-person experience. We still want to see the struggle and witness, as best we can, how a founder or a customer or a brand overcame the challenges they faced and came out on top, because we see ourselves in the struggle and relate to brands that mirror our own self-image. But in an age of collapsing trust and the ubiquitous availability of real-time information, courtesy of the full democratization of personal technology, believability and credibility are in short supply. Showing the evidence in an unscripted, in-process, and in-context fashion, where we act not as someone seeking to convince our audience but as one seeking to help explain how to interpret what our audience is seeing is more persuasive. Raw is the key to satisfying the need for rational decision-making.

PART 3

Implications

Each of the macro trends we've presented is powerful as a stand-alone concept. Each can be isolated and implemented so that it sharpens what's already in place or acts as a catalyst to spark bigger and better thinking. And far from simply pigeon-holing them as "out-bound marketing tools," we can credibly say, based on experience, that smart teams can and have implemented these insights in areas as diverse as sales, product development, human resources, and acquisition integration.

We often find that opportunities for growth are hidden in plain sight, where adding a third element can change the dynamic between the problem and the environment we find ourselves in. Like a third person entering a private conversation, sometimes the new element changes the dynamic so completely that the dialogue blooms and takes directions that never could have happened had it stayed narrowly defined between the original two people.

We find the same holds true for these key macro trends. When we view them separately, they each deliver a clear call to action for the careful student of business.

The bigger idea, though, is what happens when we combine all three ideas into a single, holistic system, where each trend reinforces and amplifies the other two.

When we view "seeking control in an out-of-control world," "raw" in its several forms, and "heroic credibility" as a single system, we see a blueprint emerge, a playbook for leaders seeking to change how work is accomplished through people in a complex enterprise.

CHAPTER 8

Implications for Leadership:
The New Blueprint

Hi, I'm Ed Bastian, CEO of Delta Airlines. I wanted to give you an update with respect to the recovery progress we're making from yesterday's system outage. . . . [1]

Ed Bastian, CEO of Delta Airlines

On August 8, 2016, a fire and subsequent power outage took thirty Delta Airlines servers offline, stranding hundreds of thousands of passengers in airports around the country. CEO Ed Bastian didn't hesitate to communicate with a nation of angry customers, going on camera via Twitter at 10:48 a.m. to give what was surely an incomplete, but partial, status update on what was happening. "I'm Ed Bastian . . . I'm speaking to you today from our operations and customer center where we've got Delta teams working around the clock to restore our systems capabilities. . . ." [2]

Bastian's lead-from-the-front-on-video approach didn't end with his 10:48 a.m. announcement, either. He once again appeared on video, this time in a slightly more relaxed and less chaotic environment, the next day to explain what had happened, what Delta was doing to compensate stranded passengers, and to put the entire event into perspective.

This instant willingness of a CEO—often in a position that we assume is above reproach and who would never admit to anything less than total omnipotence—to step in front of a camera, with a harried operations center just over his shoulder literally attempting to solve a complex IT problem as the camera rolled, is a clear example of the synthesis of raw: how the absolute alpha level of leaders look at how they can push control back to their stakeholders, communicate in raw fashion, and demonstrate heroic credibility, all in a single holistic operating system.

While Delta's 2016 IT failure was an isolated event, Bastian's response is indicative of a mindset that embraces how best to communicate to a market of customers, stakeholders, employees, and others immersed in technology and culturally attuned to a pace of change and access to the sources of information. And therein lies the big idea and the first big synthesis of these macro trends: while each is a useful tool in the hands of any leader seeking to effect change in their organization, they are far more powerful when we view them as a holistic system. Viewed together, they create a playbook for leadership in this info-immersive age.

How can today's CEO employ this playbook? Listen to Bastian again discuss how he pushes control back to his employees and communicates in an unscripted way:

> Today, with technology, you can do it better than ever. With 80,000 people, it's really hard to feel a personal relationship," says Bastian. In order to get closer to his employees, Bastian takes a novel approach. Several times a week, wherever he is in the world, he will take out his smart phone and do an internet chat with his employees. He'll explain where he is, talk about the state of the business and then take questions. "It's not high tech, it's just using my phone. And they follow you. And they understand you. They understand how you think.[3]

John Legere of T-Mobile takes a similar approach. "On my very first day at T-Mobile, I demanded that every time I spoke publicly to the company, all employees across the country would be invited to watch," Legere explained. "I faced legal and all that crap, but ultimately we were able to figure it out."[4]

This playbook reads like the wish list of every corporate employee in the workforce today.

We want leaders who find every possible way to give employees and consumers a sense of control over their outcomes. We want to see where we are in the process, on demand. We want self-sufficiency and clarity. And we want to know how things are going, directly and transparently describing how you're doing it.

We want leaders who want to move toward an immediate, transparent, work-in-process footing for brand communications. We want leaders who want to go faster, be less polished, and be more human. We're OK with leaders giving up some control—an uncomfortable amount of control, really, showing prospects, channel partners, and even competitors why your company is doing what it is doing, as well as even tipping its hand as to what the brand is working on. We want leadership that is willing to show the world (and us) how we design our products and where materials come from (right down to the farm or factory) and why we all care so damn much about what we do.

And lastly, we want to work for leaders who are willing to find out exactly how far out on that edge the culture can go without having a panic attack. We want to be part of an organization creating a movement that we and our peers will embody so that everything we do transcends a narrowly defined product category. We want to work for a company where people walk with their feet off the ground. We want leadership that makes us feel bigger than our industry. We want leadership that shouts this from the rooftops. And if the social media wolfpack gives us pushback, we want a leader who doubles down hard.

PUSHING CONTROL BACK TO THE CONSUMER AT HOME: SEEKING CONTROL AT SC JOHNSON

"We see profitability as the means for achieving success. It is *not* the success itself," says Fisk Johnson, chairman and CEO of SC Johnson, one of the world's leading manufacturers of household cleaning products and products for home storage, air care, pest control, and shoe care. The Racine, Wisconsin-based company generated $10 billion in sales in 2018 and has approximately 13,000 employees globally. "For five generations, SC Johnson has cared not just about winning, but winning the right way. We act with integrity, respect people, produce quality products, make responsible and courageous choices, and pursue growth so we can keep doing good in the world."[5]

Giving consumers a sense of control is at the very heart of the way SC Johnson does business. "Although most decisions are a matter of trade-offs and evolving priorities, one priority doesn't change for us: acting in the best interest of our customers, whose trust in our company is a primary reason they buy our products,"[6] explains Fisk Johnson. One of the ways the company does this is by being completely transparent about the ingredients that go into its products. Disclosing ingredients in household products is not required in the United States, but SC Johnson was the first to do so. The company knew that taking such a step could put it at a competitive disadvantage. However, SC Johnson also knew that consumers were concerned about the safety of the products they were buying as well as the environmental impact of the products they used. Consumers wanted a greater sense of control over their product decisions, and SC Johnson responded. More importantly, from SC Johnson's point of view, the company was doing it because it was the right thing to do.

Back in 2001, long before consumers were reading product labels and demanding environmental accountability, and long before companies were taking voluntary steps to list product ingredients on their labels, SC Johnson created a science-based, peer-reviewed program it called Greenlist, which evaluated every product ingredient's potential impact on people and the environment. The company developed a four-point scale that rated thousands of different chemicals based on safety and environmental criteria and then tracked them over time. The goal of the program was to give product developers as well as suppliers a continuously updated list of the safest and most environmentally friendly ingredients.

Several years later, the company took an additional step. Like many other companies, SC Johnson uses many kinds of fragrances in its products, and fragrances are made up of hundreds of different chemical components. SC Johnson ran every single component through its safety and environmental criteria and in the process eliminated over 2,400 out of 3,700 components. Most of those components continue to be used by other companies, but not by SC Johnson. That level of scrutiny and concern is one of the qualities that sets SC Johnson apart from its competitors.

In 2017, the company went even further, this time disclosing the presence of 368 skin allergens that may occur in its products. The action went beyond any regulations that existed in the European Union or the United States and far beyond what other manufacturers have done. Other companies use similar ingredients but have not taken similar steps.

All told, SC Johnson has shared more than 99.9 percent of the ingredients in its product formulas, setting an industry standard. "Now more than ever," says Fisk Johnson, "consumers demand transparency from brands, and we always try to be one step ahead to lead the industry to higher standards. [We want to] give consumers what they need to make the best choices for their families."[7]

SC Johnson earns good will and trust by being transparent and giving consumers the information they need to make good purchasing decisions. It also is transparent because, like Levi Strauss in chapter 5, SC Johnson is guided by a set of values that go back to the company's founder, Samuel Curtis Johnson. In 1927, he said in a speech: "Good will is the only enduring thing in any business. It is the sole substance. The rest is shadow."[8]

TRACEABILITY ON DEMAND, VIA THE SMARTPHONE IN YOUR POCKET: RAW AT SC JOHNSON

SC Johnson also demonstrates the tenets of raw through its traceability programs. The company knows that consumers want to know where their products come from, how they are made, and who makes them. "When you buy one of our products, you put your trust in us," the company says on its website. "That is a responsibility we take seriously. We put our family name on every product we make, because we stand behind every product as only a family company can."[9]

Full traceability is an important part of the trust equation, and SC Johnson addresses it by providing consumers with extensive information on its manufacturing facilities and the products that are made there. For example, the company's Waxdale facility near its headquarters in Racine, Wisconsin, produces sixteen different products and 60 million cases of product each year, and it is the largest and fastest single-site aerosol manufacturer in the world, producing 430 million aerosol cans each year. The main facility is three-quarters of a mile long, and its buildings cover 2.2 million square feet—about the size of thirty-six American football fields. The facility is also an example of the company's sustainability commitment, with most of the massive facility powered by two giant 415-foot wind turbines and a cogeneration system that uses waste methane gas from a nearby landfill.

The company has also created a recycling traceability program. In 2018, it expanded its sustainability efforts by announcing a major commitment to address the growing plastic waste crisis around the world. It is working with industry and nonprofit organizations in a number of countries where it does business to develop circular plastic economy models. These systems are designed to encourage recycling and create a recycling chain that consolidates all recyclables, sells them to recyclers, and guarantees that the materials at the end of the process are used in "new" packaging. The entire process is traceable from smartphones so consumers can track it. SC Johnson has already begun to use the plastic coming from such programs; its first product, launched in 2019, is called Windex Vinegar Ocean Plastic.

Both efforts are excellent examples of how good companies add context to the buying decision and bring consumers closer to the companies they do business with.

MAKING THE HARD CHOICES: HEROIC CREDIBILITY AT SC JOHNSON

Does SC Johnson demonstrate heroic credibility? Is it willing to take a heroic stance on subjects it feels passionate about and then willing to stand behind them when criticism comes its way?

"We believe it is incredibly important to go above and beyond what is expected," says Fisk Johnson, "and to do our part to be an environmental and social leader."[10] Kelly Semrau, SC Johnson's senior vice president of global corporate affairs, puts it this way: "For us, doing the right thing is about being responsible, ethical and always mindful that we're part of something bigger. We aim to go beyond mere compliance and lead the way, and even to disrupt the industry at times."[11]

In the minds of many, SC Johnson's environmental commitment goes back to its preemptive and voluntary decision in 1975 to remove all chlorofluorocarbons (CFCs) from its products. Then-CEO Sam Johnson had read scientific research that suggested CFCs might harm the earth's ozone layer, and after much internal deliberation, he made the bold decision to ban CFCs from all of its aerosol products worldwide. Industry leaders accused Johnson of being irresponsible, reckless, and premature. They argued that SC Johnson should have waited until the science was settled, instead of acting on "emotion." One industry executive accused Johnson of trying to destroy the chemical industry. He said: "Sam, you're gonna ruin this industry."[12]

The decision was not easy, and it hurt the company's business in the short term. At the time, alternative propellants did not exist in many countries, and SC Johnson was forced to abandon many of its products. Nevertheless, the company stood fast by its decision, and it was a wake-up call for the industry. Several years later, the federal government acknowledged the wisdom of the SC Johnson decision and banned the use of CFCs from all products. Twenty years later, the research that Sam Johnson had used to make his decision went on to win the 1995 Nobel Prize in chemistry.

Sam Johnson set a standard for environmental responsibility that SC Johnson measures itself by today. SC Johnson has a legacy of making bold decisions to protect the environment and none more so than its 2018 commitment to minimize plastic waste. This decision is surprising, given that the company's brands include Ziploc plastic bags, Saran Wrap plastic wrap, plastic bottles of Windex, Scrubbing Bubbles, and Fantastik spray cleaners. Fisk Johnson explains: "The whole issue of plastic waste from our products going into landfills is the single biggest environmental issue for our company."[13] According to the company's website, a million plastic bottles are bought around the world every minute of every day, and very few end up being recycled. Most end up in landfills or worse. It is estimated that there are 5 trillion pieces of plastic debris in the world's oceans.[14]

Plastic waste seems like an insurmountable problem, but Fisk Johnson, like his father before him, is determined to do something about it and in the process set an example for others to follow. And just like his father's decision to eliminate CFCs, Fisk Johnson's decision to minimize the company's use of plastic has not gone over well with the plastics industry. The Plastics Industry Association—of which SC Johnson is a member—is opposed to bans on single-use plastic. "As far as the Plastics Industry Association is concerned," says Johnson, "we have been supportive of several of their initiatives; however, in the context of bans our positions diverge."[15]

SC Johnson's commitment includes ensuring 100 percent of SC Johnson plastic packaging will be recyclable, reusable, or compostable by 2025 (in 2019, the company was at 90 percent of its goal); tripling the amount of post-consumer recycled (PCR) plastic content in its packaging by 2025 (growing from 10 million kilograms of PCR plastic in 2019 to 30 million kilograms by 2025); expanding the number of concentrated refill options for its products; removing excess plastics wherever possible (from 2011 to 2017, the company removed 9.5 million kilograms of materials from its packaging); and working with the industry and nongovernmental organizations (NGOs) to support circular plastic economy models to keep plastic out of landfills and the environment.[16]

SC Johnson is an excellent example of a company whose business model is the powerful synthesis of our macro trends: "seeking control" + "raw" + "heroic credibility." SC Johnson's belief in ingredient transparency in an industry not known for its willingness to disclose the chemical make-up of its products (seeking control), its commitment to traceability in its supply chain and its recycling efforts, and its commitment to be a leader in social and environmental responsibility (heroic credibility) make SC Johnson the kind of twenty-first century company capable of keeping the trust of digitally distracted consumers.

HOW THE LEADERSHIP BLUEPRINT WORKS WHEN THINGS GO WRONG: PUTTING "SEEKING CONTROL" + "RAW" + "HEROIC CREDIBILITY" TO WORK AT DELTA AIRLINES

"I believe that when people do the right thing, they deserve to be acknowledged for it," said Amy Rees Anderson, managing partner and founder of REES Capital. "So today I want to acknowledge that Delta, under the leadership of CEO Ed Bastian, did the right thing." Anderson's remarks were in response to the way Delta personnel and the Delta CEO had handled a bad experience she had recently had while flying with Delta.

Anderson writes a blog, and she used it to express her anger about the poor customer service she had received. She said she wanted to pick up the phone and call Delta's CEO to complain. And she wondered out loud whether he would even care.

Somehow, Delta discovered the post, and almost immediately Delta CEO Ed Bastian's executive assistant, Susanna Curtis, called Anderson. Curtis explained that Ed Bastian had read her post and wanted to personally apologize for the bad experience she had had. He wanted her to know that Delta was at fault, and they were very sorry. Her experience had identified a number of issues, and changes would be made to address them. No excuses, no getting defensive. Anderson was pleasantly surprised by Delta's response. All companies will make mistakes, she wrote: "but what defines a company is the way they handle those mistakes."[17]

Anderson's customer service experience with Delta was similar to the way Bastian handled the power outage detailed at the beginning of this chapter. Bastian and his team believe in the power of raw and the importance of honesty, transparency, and authenticity in the way they do business. Since Bastian became CEO in 2016, he has become known for his unique management style and for a culture that nurtures its employees. "One of the most important things, if not the most important thing I do, is spend quality time with our people—not just at the management level, but with our frontline personnel," says Bastian. Bastian believes that the best way to be customer-centric is to be employee-centric. In talking about his leadership style, Bastian explains that he spends a lot of his time talking with his employees and making sure they have the tools they need to be successful. "You've got to make certain that your employees know that they are the absolute best asset you have," says Bastian.[18]

Delta is one of the largest and most profitable airlines in the world. However, it wasn't always that way. When Bastian took the CEO job in 2016, he was told that the company was going to be out of cash within six weeks. Its credit card providers were withholding payments and, as he put it, "People could smell blood in the water."

He had to turn the company around—and fast. That meant extracting pay cuts from everyone—pilots, frontline employees, ground crews, management—everyone. Some of those cuts were as deep as 50 percent. Employees were angry and morale plummeted. How can you say your employees are your most important asset and then treat them that way?

Bastian did what a raw CEO would do. He brought in everyone, a few hundred employees at a time, and explained everything—how the company got into this mess, what he and his team were doing, and what they were going to do. No fancy PowerPoint presentation, no complicated finance charts. Just him in front of his employees. Then a long question-and-answer period. Every question answered to the best of his ability. No dodging the tough ones. No excuses. No pinning the blame on others. And then, in a show of faith, he told the employees that if they stayed and the company was successful in turning things around, 15 percent of the profits would go to them—and go to them first. Not to the management team, not to the shareholders.[19]

The employees stuck with him, and Delta turned it around. A few years later, Delta paid out $100 million to its employees and, for the past five years, it has paid its employees over $1 billion a year in profit-sharing. Some investors groused, but Delta didn't budge. For Ed Bastian, the commitment he made to his employees was, as he put it, "sacrosanct. I talk almost in spiritual terms about it."[20]

Ed Bastian has proven that he believes in the power of raw, and by putting faith in his employees and their ability to understand and appropriately respond to the needs of Delta's customers, he has also proven that he believes in giving back control.

However, is Ed Bastian an example of a leader with heroic credibility or just an example of a strong leader who understands the importance of his employees and giving them the tools to obsess over customers? In February 2018, an event occurred that put him to the test.

On Valentine's Day, a gunman opened fire at the Marjory Stoneman Douglas High School in Parkland, Florida, killing seventeen students and staff and injuring another seventeen. It was, at the time, one of the deadliest mass shootings in American history. It reignited a national debate over gun control and galvanized many Parkland students to organize and speak out against gun violence. The Parkland students, as they came to be called, did some research on companies doing business with the National Rifle Association (N.R.A.) and learned that Delta offered N.R.A. members a travel discount. The Parkland students contacted Bastian via social media and asked him about the Delta relationship with the N.R.A.

Bastian said he was unaware of the N.R.A. relationship but he would look into it. Within a day, after consulting with a few close colleagues, he made the decision to terminate the discount. He said he made the decision because it wasn't something that provided any financial value to the company. "It wasn't an anti-N.R.A. stance or pro-gun-control stance," he told the *New York Times*.[21]

Predictably, the social media attack dogs pounced, and the press portrayed the decision as Delta taking a stance on gun control. Others saw it as a public relations stunt by a CEO with a huge ego. And some pro-N.R.A. flyers formed an organization to boycott the airline. Bastian claims that he knew there would be risks, but he hadn't expected what happened next. The Georgia legislature had recently approved eliminating a jet fuel tax that would have saved Delta over $40 million. The N.R.A., angered by the Delta decision, used its considerable lobbying power to convince the legislature to exempt Delta from the tax relief bill. All of a sudden, Delta was plunged into the political quagmire it had sought to avoid, and it was facing a $40 million hit it had not expected or planned for.

Was this a case of heroic credibility or the foolish act of a CEO acting on his own—a case of brand militancy?

As the controversy swirled, Bastian asked his communications team to draft a statement for him explaining Delta's position and the rationale behind it. However, when he read it, it didn't ring true. "What came back just wasn't my words," said Bastian. "So I threw it away and sat down and wrote it myself. And it was from my heart. It was more than a business decision for me. Our decision was not made for economic gain, and our values are not for sale."[22]

Even though he did not poll his employees—and, in fact, had not even informed his board of directors—before making the decision to drop the N.R.A. discount, he was confident that his employees stood with him.

His employees backed him, the social media storm subsided, business returned, and the Georgia legislature quietly reinstated the $40 million tax break.

In 2018, *Fortune* magazine named Bastian one of "The World's 50 Greatest Leaders," along with Bill and Melinda Gates, the presidents of France and South Korea, and Apple CEO Tim Cook. Delta was also honored with the *Fortune* "100 Best Places to Work" award for 2018.[23]

KEY TAKEAWAYS

We have seen how leaders can use each of the key macro trends to effect positive change in their organizations. When taken together, however, the combination of "seeking control" + "raw" + "heroic credibility" creates a powerful synergy and a playbook for leadership in this digitally distracted age.

How can we give consumers a sense of control?

Fisk Johnson at SC Johnson has sought to give customers control of their purchasing process by disclosing all of the ingredients the company uses in formulating its products. Further, SC Johnson analyzes and discloses the components of its fragrances and even identifies possible skin allergens that may be present in its products.

Authenticity and transparency are important company values, and Johnson uses them to help guide SC Johnson's product development decisions. He also knows that today's consumers want to do business with companies that take values like authenticity and transparency seriously.

Johnson recognizes that giving control to consumers is the best way to gain customer commitment. Brand loyalty has been replaced by customer control.

How can we give employees a sense of control?

Ed Bastian at Delta has an exemplary style of leadership that is the envy of the entire airline industry. What is his secret? He would tell you that it has nothing to do with him and everything to do with his employees. He believes in his employees and giving them the tools to meet and exceed customer needs. Instead of a hierarchical culture that focuses on internal compliance, best-practice benchmarks, and metrics that detract from customer-centricity (such as on-time departure stats versus making sure connecting passengers are able to make their connections), Delta's employees are empowered to make on-the-spot decisions and manage ambiguous situations. Delta's 80,000+ employees know that they will be rewarded for taking ownership of results rather than just completing tasks (or following a script).

Bastian's view is that the best way to meet customer needs is to meet employee needs. What sets Delta apart is its DNA, which is the spirit of the company. By giving employees a sense of control, Delta has created a company where superior customer service has become a competitive advantage.

How can we make the spirit of raw our leadership style?

In a world where we only trust what we can see with our own eyes and hear with our own ears, filtered through our own judgment, we hunger for raw. Raw is more than a set of tactics. It is a mindset that puts consumers at ease because you, as a leader, are willing to give up some control and bring consumers into your process, even when you are not sure you have all the answers. Instead of a scripted and polished press release, Ed Bastian went on Twitter in the teeth of a major computer outage to tell the world what was going on and what steps Delta was taking to solve the problem. He wasn't as articulate as he might have been had he been reading from a script, and in talking extemporaneously, he ran the risk of speaking out of turn. However, that was THE point. We want leaders who want to talk to us directly, who are willing to tell us how things are going— even when they are not going well. We want our leaders to be more human, more vulnerable, and more transparent.

The technology that makes this possible now makes this imperative—and inevitable. While the days of press releases and finely crafted presentations are not going away, increasingly, the savvy leader will gain credibility and build trust by going raw. Gone are the days when corporate leaders can hide in their wood-paneled offices dictating directives and orchestrating grand strategies from on high. From now on, the hallmark of successful leaders will be their willingness and indeed their desire to go raw.

How can we demonstrate heroic credibility?

SC Johnson does it by supporting environmental sustainability. And Levi Strauss & Co. does it by standing up for causes it believes in and empowering its employees to do the same.

Heroic credibility is the willingness of brands and leaders to live by a set of values and then, in the face of criticism, refuse to back down.

To be credible, brand actions must be in alignment with the brand's purpose and its values. Levi Strauss & Co. can support efforts to increase voter engagement because, from its very beginning, it has always been concerned about the welfare of its employees and the people in the communities where the company does business.

Consumers want companies to do more than just make a profit for their shareholders. That is what our data shows and that is why the Business Roundtable recently changed its statement of corporate purpose. However, our data also shows that consumers are not supportive of companies that take stands on social issues, only to retreat when criticism comes their way. Consumers want to support companies that take stands on social issues consistent with their company values. Patagonia can sue the federal government and not worry this decision will hurt its business because its action is consistent with its brand values.

Heroic credibility is about living your brand values—and never backing down.

CONCLUSION

Leadership in this digitally distracted world demands a new kind of leader. We want leaders who lead from the heart, who are comfortable being less polished, who are not afraid of making mistakes and showing us their imperfections. We want leaders who are personal and direct; leaders who listen more than talk; leaders who are more human.

We want leaders who are willing to give up some control, both to their employees and to their customers; leaders who are willing to show the world how they design their products and where their materials come from. We want leaders who are willing to involve consumers in their design and development process; leaders who are excited by the prospect of cocreation.

And finally, we want leaders who are heroes; leaders who live by a set a values we want to follow, who make us feel more powerful than our roles, who challenge us to make a difference in this world.

We want leaders who know how to push control to both employees and customers, who are comfortable living in a state of rawness and who demonstrate heroic credibility.

CHAPTER 9

Implications for Brand Loyalty: Operating in a State of Rawness

We gave away our sales for one day to environmental causes. The sales for that one day were [five] times what we expected. . . . It wasn't a hard decision to make. It is who we are.[1]

Rose Marcario, president and CEO of Patagonia

On Black Friday, November 25, 2018, outdoor apparel maker Patagonia did something it had never done before. It donated all its sales for that day, one of the busiest shopping days of the year, to environmental causes. The sales for that one day came in at over $10 million, five times more than a normal trading day. But Marcario was not too surprised. She believes that many of the customers that day were new to Patagonia and had decided to shop with the company because they had heard that Patagonia had sued the Trump administration over its intention to reduce the size of the Bears Ears and Grand Staircase-Escalante National Monuments in Utah.

Why did Patagonia decide to sue the federal government—a decidedly odd move for an apparel manufacturer? Because one of its core values is "Use business to protect nature."[2]

Patagonia is a firm believer in something beyond financial growth, as founder and CEO Yvon Chouinard has often said. Growth for the sake of growth pushes a company to do things that will inevitably run counter to its mission and to the best interests of its customers—not to mention the planet itself. Patagonia's mission statement makes no mention of the products it manufactures and sells, simply stating, "We're in business to save our home planet."[3] While the iconoclastic founder is firm in his belief that his brand is so far out beyond the current understanding of the market that customer feedback isn't terribly important, he is optimistic that citizens of the Earth, once educated, will make the right choices for themselves and the planet—and these choices once made will influence the corporations, who will in turn influence government to do more. Chouinard sees a virtuous circle—in other words, from pushing control back into the hands of consumers to vivid transparency and rawness in how his mission is conveyed, all the way to a truly heroically credible call to action.

Chouinard and Patagonia represent one of the better examples of the true brand/consumer relationship in a technologically immersed age, which is ironic, given his personal anti-technology bent. Chouinard's product development philosophy of building products that last and can be repaired mirrors the product management philosophy of limiting the number of styles the company produces, all with the intention of simplifying, of making less stuff.

As with the leadership examples in the preceding chapter, here we see Patagonia bringing the key macro trends together in a single, holistic system that supports this amplified idea of the brand/consumer relationship and a smart vision for brand loyalty.

Patagonia's vision is to educate consumers on what quality looks like, how responsible garments are made, and how consumers can be stewards of both the earth and their belongings, pushing control back into the hands of the buying public. For consumers looking to regain some sense of control over their lives—from making a statement about environmental stewardship to personal sustainability—Chouinard and Patagonia provide a road map.

THE FOOTPRINT CHRONICLES: SEEKING CONTROL AT PATAGONIA

Patagonia goes further than any apparel manufacturer in providing the customer with its entire supply chain. The company details every part of the process—from the fields where its cotton is grown and the sheep farms that supply wool to the textile mills and factories where its products are made to its efforts at recycling and reusing its products.

We have chronicled how Levi Strauss & Co. and SC Johnson have taken similar steps, but Patagonia stands apart—a true global leader in supply chain transparency.

On its website, Patagonia has a map of the world with the locations of all of its farms, textile mills, and factories. It calls the map "Supply Chain: The Footprint Chronicles," and this map is a detailed explanation of everything the company is doing in its supply chain to live up to its mission statement: "We are in business to save our planet earth." For example, all of the down insulation used in its products is traceable. That means the down can be traced from the farm to the factory, and the path helps ensure the welfare of the animals. In 2018, Patagonia became the first outdoor apparel brand to be certified to the Advanced Global Traceable Down Standard, the highest level of certification possible. As the company says on its website: "Building a long-lasting product that helps you stay warm in good conscience is a legacy of which we are very proud."[4]

"The Footprint Chronicles" details everything from its recycling efforts, its Fair Trade Certified program, its commitment to solving the problem of microfibers shredding from synthetic materials, to how it is battling the climate crisis and a list of all of its finished goods suppliers. No other firm goes to such lengths to educate consumers and give them control of the purchase decision process. "The consumer has all the power," Chouinard says. "If you can educate the consumer, I think they'll make the right choices."[5]

"NO RAINBOW TROUT ON MARS": RAW AT PATAGONIA

The way Patagonia explains every detail of its supply chain is a vivid example of raw in-process and raw in-context. And Patagonia's founder and chairman is the epitome of our unscripted leader. Chouinard, like John Legere at T-Mobile and Ed Bastian at Delta Airlines, is passionate about his company and its mission. Chouinard is fighting for a more sustainable way forward, and he is not afraid of taking on other leaders he sees as being wrong-headed. In an interview he did with *Fast Company* magazine, he was asked what he thought of Jeff Bezos and Elon Musk pursuing interplanetary travel to the moon and Mars. Chouinard said: "I think it is pretty silly. And not just silly, but it's really a shame. . . . We're just wasting this money going to Mars. I want to start doing some T-shirts that just have a rainbow trout on it, the T-shirt, and it says, THERE'S NO RAINBOW TROUT ON MARS, or SCREW MARS. We gotta do that."[6] Chouinard speaking from the heart and living his values. Chouinard operating in a state of rawness.

"THE PRESIDENT STOLE YOUR LAND": HEROIC CREDIBILITY AT PATAGONIA

All of the brand's actions, products, and values are rooted in a message that transcends the narrow confines of the product category they happen to compete in. One could no more limit Patagonia's enterprise to "apparel" than one could reduce Chouinard himself to being a mountain climber. Patagonia is a perennial mainstay on lists of most respected companies and most innovative brands because it has always lived its mission statement. Patagonia *is* heroic credibility.

We need look no further than the brand's advertising, exhorting the reader, "Don't buy this jacket," a campaign that seemingly broke from the mainstream mission of selling more stuff that virtually every brand in business today naturally follows. The overt message is simple: don't buy more stuff because you're bored or for purely aesthetic reasons. But when you need one, buy the right jacket—one made right, made with quality and with respect for the planet—and wear it until it wears out. Then get it repaired.

Similarly, Chouinard and Patagonia's suit against the government over Bears Ears and Grand Staircase-Escalante National Monuments—animated by a print campaign stating, "The President Stole Your Land"—thrust the brand into the political and social sphere where it strongly believed it belonged. Again, based on everything the founder and brand have articulated on the subject, this lawsuit was anything but a PR stunt. Chouinard is famously ambivalent about customer insight. This decision is an expression of the brand's core values. It also happens to hit the bull's-eye of its customers' values as well.

THE EVOLUTION OF BRAND LOYALTY:
FROM RATIONAL TO EMOTIONAL

The impact of getting this holistic system right means greater brand loyalty, higher revenues, and an elevated valuation. The key financial benefit to this synthesis as it relates to "operating in a state of rawness" is sharper corporate strategy and execution, which covers the entire spectrum of business activities in which the enterprise is engaged. This total alignment drives greater financial performance across the enterprise, from revenue to valuation.

Patagonia—and its execution of raw—is an example of brand loyalty unlike the definition of brand loyalty we have become accustomed to. The premise behind brand loyalty has always been the same. If customers find products that deliver as promised, they will stay with them; they will be loyal to them. As long as the price/value comparison makes sense and another competitor doesn't come along with a much lower price, consumers will purchase the product year in and year out.

The culture, however, began to change and consumer buying habits shifted as well. Tried and true began to give way to new and different, and comparison shopping put brand loyalty at risk. In fear of losing market share, brands responded with loyalty programs—incentives to keep customers in the brand. If you were an airline, you offered free flights after so many miles flown. If you were a retailer, you might hold special loyalty events where loyalty card holders received special treatment and discounts. If you were a grocery store, you gave a discount to all loyalty card members. If you were a car rental company, you would offer free rentals. And so on.

Over time, loyalty programs became more sophisticated, offering tiered reward systems, charging upfront fees for VIP benefits, partnering with other companies, and providing all-inclusive offers. Most of these programs—then and now—have one thing in common: they are transaction-based and cater to rational considerations in the buying process.

All was well and good until 2015, when a research report from Capgemini, the consulting firm, revealed a problem—a big problem. Loyalty programs were no longer working. Capgemini found that 90 percent of customers have a negative perception of loyalty programs.[7] Later research, in 2017 and 2018, identified additional problems. Over half (54 percent) of loyalty memberships have lapsed, and over a quarter (28 percent) of consumers abandon loyalty programs without redeeming any points.[8] And a 2018 Maritz study learned that 68 percent of consumers identified themselves as transient brand loyalists—meaning, if a better brand came along, they would switch.[9]

What had happened? Research from various sources found that the path to sustained loyalty needs to take into consideration more than rational considerations, such as price, promotions, same-day delivery, and loyalty points. The research discovered that loyalty is a combination of three factors: rational elements, brand values, and emotions.

The research uncovered a surprise: rational considerations are not the dominant factor in customer loyalty. Emotions are the main driver of loyalty. Rational considerations come in second, and brand values come in a close third. Among the three, the correlation between emotions and loyalty is by far the strongest.[10] The key take-away from the research: to gain customers and keep them, you must address *all* three factors.

The third factor, brand values (which correlates very closely with rational considerations), consists of such business practices as being ethical, being environmentally friendly, and being socially responsible. As we have discussed, consumers identify with the brands they buy, and if their values coincide with the values of the brand, a strong bond is formed—much stronger than the connection formed through rational benefits. We have profiled a number of value-driven companies in these pages—Levi Strauss & Co., SC Johnson, Delta, and, of course, Patagonia.

The factor that has received the least attention but is most closely correlated with brand loyalty is emotions. And that makes sense. Human beings are emotional animals. It is widely believed that a vast majority of our decisions are impacted or even dictated by our emotions. And the decisions consumers make concerning brands are no different. Brands are not humans, but consumers relate to them as if they were.

The new research came as a revelation to most companies because they were working under the assumption that brand loyalty was entirely driven by rational considerations. If they got those right—right price, right selection, a good loyalty points program and the like—customers would stay with them. This point of view was buttressed by our current obsession with behavioral metrics and balanced scorecards. The joy of rational considerations—like customer churn rates, spending per transaction, and repeat purchase ratios—is that they are easy to measure and easy to track. And as the old saying goes: we measure what we value and value what we measure. Once we committed to a measurement system, our behavior conformed to it—for better or worse.

The problem, of course, is that when brands become fixated on rational considerations, it is easy to lose sight of the bigger picture.

When the research identified emotions and brand values as considerations that were either just as important or even more important than what they were measuring, most companies were unsure how to respond. And, in fact, most have not responded.

What the research revealed was that while rational considerations were important to attract new customers and, in many cases, were the reason customers left brands, rational drivers were not the main reasons why customers stayed with brands. Emotions have the greatest impact on brand loyalty. Consumers are attracted to brands they view as honest or trustworthy; have integrity; give them a sense of belonging; make them feel secure, joyous, or grateful; show compassion; and, every now and again, surprise them. That's a rank order of the emotions that have the greatest influence on loyalty.[11] Honesty, trust, and integrity top the list of qualities for building a loyal following. Further, once consumers become customers, they want a two-way relationship. They want brands to reach out to them, *and* they want brands to listen to them. When customers are asked to provide feedback—like satisfaction with their last transaction—they expect brands to act on that feedback and give them the research results. Further, they want to know how the results will be used. In chapter 8, Ed Bastian of Delta Airlines did that, responding promptly to a customer complaint, identifying possible causes, and explaining in detail how Delta was going to address the issues identified. However, how many other companies can you name that go to such lengths? It's usually a one-way street. Brands want the data—because it is one of their performance metrics—but they don't follow up. Such one-way behavior does nothing to build the relationship with their customers and can potentially damage it. What an irony: doing a customer satisfaction survey could actually hurt customer satisfaction.

Customers also expect brands to be responsive and understanding, and they want to be treated as individuals. Customers know that brands are gathering all kinds of data on them, and thus, they have come to expect that brands will use that data to benefit them. They expect brands to know their personal preferences, know their purchase history, give them exclusive offers based on their preferences, and, every now and again, surprise them with a gift to say thank you for their loyalty. Further, they are concerned about their privacy and expect brands to be careful and respectful with their data. Recall that honesty and trust are the top two drivers of sustainable brand loyalty.

Finally, just like good friendships, customers expect brands to be predictable, consistent, and reliable. Amazon is the oft-used example. When Amazon says that your package will arrive tomorrow afternoon, you count on it to keep its promise. If, for some reason, the package does not arrive on time, Amazon knows it has to make right on its promise—immediately. Trust is built on predictability, consistency, and reliability.

In this changed consumer environment, brands face a massive challenge. If loyalty is important to them, they must begin the process of shifting their relationship with their customers from a purely transactional base to an engagement base that takes into account the desire of consumers to commit to brands that share their values and to developing emotional connections that have the potential to create sustained brand loyalty. Most companies have the customer data they need to begin this process. The trick will be using the data at the right time, in the right way, and with the right intent. It is an unprecedented opportunity. Some brands will recognize and seize the opportunity.

THE FUTURE OF BRAND LOYALTY IS UNSCRIPTED, IN-PROCESS, AND IN-CONTEXT

The research identified some of the reasons why brand loyalty programs have run into difficulty, but it did not address the underlying causes. Why are loyalty programs less effective *now*? Why is more brand switching going on? Why do consumers want brands to act more like humans? What is driving consumers to seek brands that are environmentally friendly and socially responsible?

The answers to those questions have been the subject of this book. The concept of raw addresses the underlying causes and provides a pathway to the future.

As we have discussed, we are living in an age of collapsing trust. The only thing we now trust is what we can see with our own eyes and hear with our own ears. We don't want news commentators, pundits, or PR flacks telling us what to believe. We are inundated with fake news, false narratives, corporate scandals, and reports that our smart devices are spying on us. In this environment, is it any wonder that the recent research on brand loyalty has identified trust as one of the most important elements in building and sustaining brand loyalty?

We want the raw feed and the livestream. We want the CEO on camera in the middle of a crisis giving us a live update on what is happening. We know that the world as presented in the media and in corporate news releases is not the real world, and we are tired of it. We want complete visibility and direct access. No middlemen, no corporate spin doctors, no third-party interpretation.

We want the raw evidence so we can evaluate it in our own way, through our own experience and from our own point of view. The more unfiltered, the more unadulterated, the better. We want the truth. And again, that is what the recent research on brand loyalty revealed. Honesty was identified as the most important quality in building and sustaining brand loyalty. We want the facts. And we want them unscripted.

Consumers are also interested in the backstory. Since they begin every brand relationship with the assumption that they are going to be lied to or in some way deceived, they are looking for evidence that your brand can be trusted. They are interested in learning as much as possible so they can judge for themselves whether you can be trusted. Therefore, they are interested in your brand's history and pedigree. They want to know: how is your product made, where is it made, who makes it, and how do you treat the people who make it? Does your manufacturing process damage the environment? Are you a socially responsible company? What are your company values?

The more consumers know, the greater the chance they will be able to trust what they are buying. And the more they know, the greater the chance they will become loyal to you and your brand. Further, because they know your backstory and have taken the time to learn the facts and dig into the details, they are no longer consumers; they have become brand experts. They have come to know your brand. And that generates an important benefit.

Consumers who know your backstory will have a great story to tell, and chances are, they will tell others. By focusing on the backstory—giving consumers a history of your brand, showing them where and how your product was made—as we profiled in the chapter 4 case study of Gold'n Plump poultry's Just BARE brand—brands have a powerful opportunity to turn customers into brand advocates. Everyone loves a good story, and a rich brand story is one of the best ways to generate strong word-of-mouth advertising, which is the best kind of advertising.

Integrity is very important to consumers (the number-three quality consumers are looking for in brands, as identified in the research), and by telling your origin story and being transparent about every step in your supply chain, you go a long way toward showing consumers that you are a brand with integrity. This is raw in-process.

We now know that emotions are the main driver of brand loyalty, and the top three drivers of emotions—honesty, trustworthiness, and integrity—are the very essence of raw.

CONSUMERS WILL COMMIT TO YOU IF YOU COMMIT TO THEM

The recent customer loyalty studies have also found that customers want more than an emotional connection and a shared-values connection to brands. They also expect a two-way relationship. Earlier we talked about the importance of responding to customers if they provided you with information you wanted, such as filling out a customer satisfaction study. However, they expect considerably more. They expect "unprecedented levels of care, responsiveness, contextual awareness, personalization, and helpfulness."[12]

Building this connection begins by recognizing that customers want brands to treat them as if they were friends. Of course, they know that brands will never be friends, but what they want is the kind of connection they have with friends. They want real-time responses, multiple ways to interact with you, and they want the relationship to be dynamic. When they change, they expect you to change your response (contextual awareness). When they comment on your new brand offering or your new marketing campaign, they expect you to appreciate their thoughtfulness. When they have a complaint, they expect you to respond promptly, understanding the context of the issue and then resolving it in a professional manner. They expect the relationship to be a two-way street, one built on responsiveness, respect, and recognition.

Companies on top of their game, the real leaders in the field of customer loyalty, understand that their customers want even more. They want the dynamic between the brand and the consumer to fundamentally change. Remember here that we now live in a C2B world where the customer is in charge, not the brand. And as such, no amount of trying to cater to the evolving needs of the consumer from the perspective of the brand will do. As long as you, as the brand owner, are in charge of the dynamic, no amount of sensitivity to the consumer will *ever* be enough. It is a losing battle because you can no longer dictate the terms of customer engagement; only the customer can do that.

Customers want to be treated like equals. Instead of being asked how much they like your new product, they want to be involved in the process of its creation and development. They want to be insiders, invited into the tent and asked to participate in the product development process.

As we noted in chapter 3, if consumers are invited to be active participants in the design and development process, they will likely tell their friends and, because of their involvement, they are more likely to support your final product. They will feel a sense of belonging and a connection to you that is far more powerful than being asked to send feedback on a product that has already launched. And it is far more engaging than the transactional benefits of most brand loyalty programs.

Most companies do not yet bring consumers into the initial phase of the product development process (where concepts are dreamt up and prototypes developed), because there are too many trade secrets and intellectual property issues involved. However, a good deal of experimentation is going on in what is being called *lean innovation*. In lean innovation, consumers are brought into the process right after the prototype stage. MillerCoors, for example, has an online panel of 10,000 consumers that it uses to test possible brand names and new beverage flavors.[13] In a similar fashion, Procter & Gamble Co. (P&G) gets consumers involved early by going online with digital ads for conceptual products.[14] If a concept tests well, the company will make a small batch of real products and sell them online—just like a start-up might do. For huge companies like MillerCoors and P&G, this new kind of product development process is nothing short of revolutionary. It overturns decades of established innovation practices. However, the real pay-off for them is not just faster speed-to-market or radically decreased product development costs; the real pay-off is a dramatically changed relationship with consumers and the building of a new kind of brand loyalty based on the in-process principle of raw.

Perhaps even more exciting is the concept of cocreation we feature in chapter 3. Adidas flips the traditional product development process on its head and almost entirely eliminates the boundaries between brand and user. The adidas product development philosophy of "swimming in the culture" takes the MillerCoors and P&G innovations one giant step further. Adidas brings consumers into its studio, shows them how the company goes about developing products, and then gives the consumers the tools they need to create *with* adidas designers. Instead of asking consumers for their input, adidas views product development as cocreation—adidas and consumers together. It is an exciting process that keeps adidas on top of the latest trends and in the process creates brand evangelists. And what's better than brand loyalty? Brand evangelism.

In chapter 3, we also tell the story of Emily Weiss and the creation of Glossier, the multimillion-dollar start-up. It's an extraordinary story that obliterates everything we thought we knew about how product development works. Glossier is not the result of a product development process but rather the product of the collective desires of consumers. Glossier uses its blog of over 10 million readers to solicit ideas and suggestions for new products. It always starts with a question, like the one that actually started it all: "What's Your Dream Cleanser?" It then uses the input it receives, along with real-life listening, to create new products. It is the kind of product development process that could never have happened without today's technology, and it is vivid proof of what happens when you use the technology to put the consumer at the center of the product development process. There is reason to believe that someday most product development will be done this way, and when that day comes, no one will worry about brand loyalty because the consumers themselves were the creators of the brand. At that point, the concept of brand loyalty as we have known it will cease to exist.

KEY TAKEAWAYS

Given what we have learned about the evolution of brand loyalty and its current state, how can we put these lessons to work? Using the lessons of raw, how can we strengthen our relationship with our customers?

What cultural changes would we need to make to become a values-driven company? Is it even worth considering?

Patagonia's vision to educate consumers on what quality looks like, how responsible garments are made, and how consumers can join them in being stewards of the Earth represents a new way to connect with consumers and strengthen brand loyalty. It is based on a concept of shared values, and it is becoming increasingly important because it resonates with younger consumers. How could we build a culture of shared values? What can we learn from our founding documents and our company history that we could use to develop a set of values we could live by? Does our long-range strategy fit with a values-driven vision? What can we learn from companies like Patagonia and Levi Strauss & Co.?

What steps do we need to take to take to strengthen our current brand loyalty program?

We know that to be in the game, we need to deliver on the basics— product quality, price competitiveness, customer service, on-time delivery, an easily navigated website, a strong loyalty points program, and relevant promotions/offers. Are we delivering on the basics? Do we understand how our customers view us? What do they tell us about our strengths and weaknesses? We need to be brutally honest with ourselves. No blaming others or making excuses. If we were beginning today, how would we do things differently?

How can we develop a deeper emotional bond with our customers?

We know that emotional connections drive brand loyalty. Does anyone say that they love us or adore us? Have our customers told us that our relationship with them makes them happy? Do these kinds of questions make us squeamish? If so, we need to identify the reasons and address them as soon as possible. Honesty, trust, and integrity top the list as the most important qualities in strong and enduring customer relationships. We should make it a priority to identify all touchpoints in our customers' journey and ask, at each point, does this interaction consistently build trust, or does it put us in jeopardy? What steps can we take to give our customers a sense of belonging? What can we do to make them feel secure? And how can we show them that we are grateful for their support?

How can we use the power of raw to rethink and recalibrate our loyalty program?

Raw means unscripted, in-process, and in-context. Unscripted builds trust. In-process brings customers into the product development process and turns them into brand advocates, and in-context makes customers coequal partners in the development process and turns them into brand evangelists. When combined, they create a synergy that redefines the concept of brand loyalty. Raw creates a strong and enduring emotional bond with customers that builds and maintains trust, is responsive to their changing needs, and is built on a foundation of shared values.

We should ask ourselves these questions: Should we rethink our current brand loyalty program? Are we ready to embrace the power of raw?

CONCLUSION

Raw redefines the brand/consumer relationship. The power of raw comes from flipping the polarity from the brand to the consumer and putting the consumer at the center of everything we do. Brand loyalty programs are at a critical juncture because they no longer meet the needs of technologically immersed consumers in this age of collapsing trust. Nevertheless, consumers' interest in committing to brands remains; witness the experience of Patagonia.

However, to meet the needs of today's consumer, we need to focus our attention on their emotional needs and their desire to partner with brands that share their values. Consumers will commit to us when we commit to them. For brand loyalty, raw is a new path forward.

CHAPTER 10

Implications for Culture: Control, Rawness, and Heroism @ Work

There's only one truth. You can't have a brand truth that's inside your company in one that's outside your company. We market to our employees first, tell them that we're going to be incredibly consistent, tell them they can do it, start hiring people that demonstrate this stuff, and then promote the people inside the company that demonstrate this stuff.

Blake Irving, former GoDaddy CEO,
in an interview with the author on October 1, 2019

First, let's acknowledge that cultural change is hard. Cultures—at least in those organizations that truly have cultures—are rooted in the collective years of relationships between coworkers, the supervisor-subordinate relationship, the rewards and punishments systems, and everything that lives in the white space between meetings, performance reviews, and informal conversations in the hall. Changing these forms requires that long-established rituals and expectations be broken—and sometimes, not everyone is on board with the breaking process.

However, with a proper blueprint that is rooted in the intersection of modern culture and the technological environment it operates in, we have a defined path upon which we can embark that follows the topography of the current culture we operate in; this way, we have a fighting chance of being successful in shifting the culture at work to a more productive, inviting, and profitable course.

The story of Blake Irving's tenure at GoDaddy provides us with an example we can model when we try to go down this path ourselves.

HOW TO CHANGE A CULTURE: THE GODADDY STORY

Any discussion of GoDaddy, the world's premier domain registrar, needs to start with its iconoclastic and larger-than-life founder, Bob Parsons. The gruff, volatile ex-Marine founded a company and a culture very much in his own image. GoDaddy was famous for its advertising, featured on the Super Bowl each year, replete with scantily clad women and a somewhat sophomoric creative strategy that skirted the edge of taste and propriety. Each year, the advertising community would collectively sniff that the company had finally gone too far, with *AdWeek*'s Barbara Lippert famously stating that the company was, in the opinion of the professional advertising intelligentsia, the lowest of the low.

Regardless, Parsons relished his time in the spotlight each year, welcoming the criticism, stating at one point that he'd rather the public hate his advertising than love it, because the emotional investment needed to have such a strong opinion would ultimately draw more attention to the brand. Indeed, he once confided that after a particularly well-orchestrated letter-writing campaign demanding that he stop his salacious advertising, he had a team member do an analysis on new domain registrations and found that many of those who had penned these critical letters had, in fact, ultimately become customers. GoDaddy was the only game in town, the only domain registrar that anyone could think of by brand name. Whether you loved it or hated it, you always looked there first to register your new domain.

Parsons was on a roll, promoting his company with his personality, and showing that you, too, could have the same kind of fun by being your own boss and launching your own website.

If the company embodied the founder's outsized persona in its marketing, the internal culture matched it as well. The culture was a top-down hierarchy, with Parsons calling the shots and his people charged more with execution than thinking for themselves. Employees from entry level to the C-suite signed timecards. Some areas of the campus were off-limits to everyone but senior management, protected by armed security guards and locked doors. And while the former CEO was admittedly irreverent, funny, and personally engaging, the culture itself was rooted in fear. Parsons fired people quickly. And as a result, people didn't speak up, and no one really spoke about what was on their minds. Employees were prohibited from personalizing their cubicles. The dress code stipulated no shorts, no hats, and no flip flops.

All this in a tech company located in Arizona.

DISARM AND ASSAIL: PUSHING CONTROL BACK INTO THE HANDS OF THE PEOPLE

The culture Blake Irving walked into at GoDaddy in 2013 could be quickly described as one where no one was trusted to do the right thing. All policies and procedures were built around this central premise that the company needed to put safeguards around everything—business processes as well as physical facilities, dress codes, and everything else—to ensure that bad actors couldn't do bad things. As a result, the culture was deeply rooted in fear. This was the first thing Irving decided to change.

"Disarm and assail" was what Irving called his playbook, working to undo the fear-based culture and instill a sense of trust in the employee base and to personally ensure that he not only mirrored the right behaviors but actively addressed things that were clearly detrimental to cultural cohesion. By assailing these unpopular cultural issues, he undid the defensiveness that he inherited. "By assailing these things myself, I disarmed the room," Irving explained. "So, you know what I'd do? I'd go to the call centers wearing shorts, flip flops, and a hat, basically saying, 'Look, we're a different company now . . . we're going to run this like a tech company in the Valley.' And by the way, the worst dressed guy in the room is often the smartest guy in the room. That's the kind of company that I think we want to be."

Another key to creating the culture of trust and of providing employees with a means to control their own outcomes is giving them a model of what the future looks like. The fastest way to change a culture is to hire it—to hire the people who think and act and communicate and collaborate the way you want your company to be and then let the legacy employee base either live up to this new model of behavior or let them ultimately find another culture that suits them better. Irving summarizes this point well, saying, "You know, you can change the culture pretty hard, you can flip it in another direction, but you need advocates that are big believers . . . it's really difficult to shift the company without some people from outside with a different perspective." Irving's first month prior to physically arriving on-site at GoDaddy was spent on the phone recruiting his dream team of the right sorts of people to help him achieve this dramatic shift in both capabilities and culture. He managed to land all of his desired candidates, which not only helped move the culture in the direction he knew it needed to go but also shored up the functional capabilities of the team and moved it closer to the "tech company in the Valley" model he envisioned. And it was this core of new executives in the building—from Microsoft, Amazon, Yahoo!, and other tech companies in the image of which Irving wanted to recast GoDaddy—that brought this new model of behavior and attitude to life.

As the human elements of the plan—the people themselves, bringing their own unique talents and characteristics to this new environment—came together, Irving turned his attention to the functional side of the culture. GoDaddy's once rigid top-down, command-and-control style went through a complete polarity flip, giving way to a new management playbook that pushed control into the hands of team leaders. Gone were the days of employees passively standing by, awaiting orders. The new regime wanted individual owners building their own strategies, defining their own milestones, and figuring out the action plans down to the most minute detail.

"We basically took individuals in the company, or people that were not yet in the company, and said, 'OK, this is your area, you write out the details on what's the strategy and what the action plan should be,' and then my job is to go get it funded by the board," Irving explained. "'And then once you're funded by the board, it's your job to get it done. And you're accountable for the metrics that you put into this plan. OK, everybody ready? Go!'"

Where once the company's strategic direction came from the founder and his unique style of coming up with ideas and having his team go execute his vision, now there was a formalized strategy, a formalized structure, and specific accountability behind each of the company's new strategic "containers" of expertise and focus.

The shift from top-down to bottom-up is a strong example of control being pushed back into the hands of the employees—employees who, for the most part, outside the new executives brought in to help effect the turnaround, had never had any sense of control before. By empowering key employees and giving them complete ownership of a critical area of the business, Irving tapped into the hunger for control in what could have easily felt like a capricious workplace. There is a holistic sense of closure, of having control of all the moving parts, when one is handed ownership of a business and is given free rein to develop the goals, milestones, strategies, and tactical plans to accomplish the task. It also requires a significant degree of trust on both parts—from the management and the employee. This, alone, likely represented a sizable part of the cultural change buy-in, as trust was decidedly lacking in years past.

GETTING YELLED AT BY DIRECT REPORTS:
RAW MEANS OPEN DOORS, ACCESSIBILITY,
AND A BIT OF HUMILITY

As we've discussed before, there is a causal relationship between the need for control, the collapse of trust, and the shift to raw. When we don't trust the institutions around us, whether it's the government or the company we work for, the only thing we believe is what we see with our own eyes and hear with our own ears. We trust our judgment when all else has failed us. So, too, with corporate culture. In an environment marked by locked doors, top-down dictates, and an impersonal view toward employees as human beings, words alone would have rung hollow. As a result, Irving's "disarm and assail" strategy of calling out the unpopular policies of the past was certainly a necessary first step, but a step nonetheless. Not only did the employee base need to hear the words and see some degree of follow-through, but they also needed to see evidence that what was being overtly "assailed" wasn't the only reason to believe in this new culture. They needed to see the small things, lived out in the everyday interactions that make up a culture.

Indeed, Irving tells of legacy direct reports who had answered to the previous CEO and lived in fear of him finally blowing up and losing his cool. Convincing many of them that they were living in a new age took a long time. "I had to pull (this employee) aside because they were just super nervous around me all the time," Irving related. "I had to go, 'Look, the guy that you keep waiting to show up doesn't exist. I just don't have it in me. This is all you get right here.'"

The effect of the new hires to the company and their natural interactions with the CEO was perhaps the most profound driver of cultural change. Again, as we've discussed, one of the more effective ways to shift a culture is to hire it—to bring in the kind of people and the kind of thinking you want in a culture and then let others either model this new behavior or choose to leave—so the impact of the new employees was critical. And it was decidedly not the deferential relationship that many had seen in previous years.

Irving described a direct report meeting with a mix of legacy and new executives around the table, where one of his new technical executives challenged him—an unheard-of act to many. "I said something that was kind of dumb or something," Irving recalled. "I don't even remember what the comment was. (A new senior executive) said, 'That is so f---ing dumb—I can't believe you even said it.' And I said, 'Oh, yeah, you know, you're right. I guess that doesn't make any sense whatsoever.' And I started laughing. But the look of horror on everyone in the room's face when he said it! It was just so funny to me. Like, Oh, my God, people are really freaking out that the guy just challenged me! And I just thought, 'OK, I get it. I know what these people were going through.'"

There's nothing so illuminating about a company's culture as watching how senior managers accept pushback from team members. In some cultures, this behavior is acceptable, but only behind closed doors and in private. In others, open clashes and chaos are the norm. And in others, they say such clashes are welcome, but it's clear from the internal backchannel that they aren't. Irving showed, without having to write a policy or articulate the idea in an all-employees meeting, that it was perfectly acceptable to speak up when anyone disagreed—even to the new boss.

From changing the unwritten rules on what was OK to say to the boss to removing the locks and barriers that separated workers from management to just showing up occasionally at the contact centers wearing shorts and flip flops, Irving modeled the behavior he expected from others on the team, showing them what was expected and proving by his actions that he meant what he said about changing the culture at GoDaddy.

Big aha moments like this one are illustrative of the bigger change, but this event was only witnessed by the people in the room. If everyone doesn't see it, does it really matter?

The day-to-day actions and interactions, boringly consistent over time, are what shift a company's culture from one place to the next. Irving described a calendar filled with one-on-one meetings, one-on-many meetings, conducted on biweekly or monthly bases. He asked participants to tell stories about themselves in an effort to break the ice and forge deeper personal relationships and break down the formality they had been so used to. In monthly town hall meetings, Irving would describe the current situation of the company, how it was doing, and what its objectives were. The goal was not just to keep people informed; it was to change the perception of the brand to its internal stakeholders—the employees themselves.

"There's only one truth," Irving related. "You can't have a brand truth that's inside your company in one that's outside your company. We market to our employees first, tell them that we're going to be incredibly consistent, tell them they can do it, start hiring people that demonstrate this stuff, and then promote the people inside the company that demonstrate this stuff. And then we just got on a cadence of communication that was very, very regimented inside the company. And when I say regimented, I know it sounds like, you know, boots marching, but it felt very organic."

This unfiltered, unscripted daily and weekly communication helped create a new perception of what the office of the CEO was like and how the company itself should act. This is how raw looks inside a company, particularly one in the throes of a massive, irreversible cultural shift.

VALUES, ASPIRATIONS, AND IPOS: HEROIC CREDIBILITY

The last key element of the framework is heroic credibility—the combination of values alignment, bold messaging, and aspiration, providing a rallying cry and beacon for both employees and customers alike. In GoDaddy's case, the company was in need of something more profound than its bad-boy brand image by the time 2013 had come around.

The company's management had come down squarely in favor of the Stop Online Piracy Act (SOPA) in 2011, something the developer community that made up the core of the company's legacy and newly hired employees were dead set against. And while the advertising campaigns that featured scantily clad women in somewhat suggestive situations were never quite as bad as they were made out to be, they rubbed people inside the company the wrong way.

Then came the elephant hunt. A 2011 video showing the former CEO hunting and killing an elephant in Zimbabwe sparked considerable internet outrage, further exacerbating tensions in the tech community and within the company.

Coming off these hits to the brand, GoDaddy needed a reset—and one that transcended creative strategies and Super Bowl ads.

"The company was in pretty bad shape towards the back end of 2012," Irving said. "My job was to come in and reinvigorate it, give it more energy, and give it a new purpose. So we focused on product, we focused on our customers, and we made sure that our messaging was around what they were doing. We tried to keep that edginess and that sort of rebel sense of humor intact, but just not directed towards women."

Irving, along with his communications team, crafted a new vision for the company around radically shifting the global economy toward small business. "If we give people tools to start their own business, when large companies start to fail, which economically always happens, we'll make it easy for people to start their own thing," Irving said. "We won't be the only people that helped this shift—it will be everybody—but we're going to be the first to actually go focus on it."

Advertising, too, took on a radically different tone. Gone were the girls. Gone was the heavy-handed creative that made half the country roll their eyes. In its place was humor—funny customers trying to get stuff done. Instead of pro wrestling diva Candice Michelle, bra strap flying, we saw Jean-Claude van Damme doing the splits, bongo drums in hand, inspiring our baker to heights of order-fulfilling and customer-service greatness, all because our hero (the baker, not Jean-Claude) had the foresight to buy a domain from GoDaddy and start down the road of customer outreach. It's Go Time, indeed. Humor and aspiration, not giggling eye candy for college kids, now positioned the brand for a new generation of small business owners looking to drive their company to the next plateau of growth.

The last major proof point came in 2015, when Irving led the IPO that took GoDaddy public, fulfilling the promise he had made to newly hired employees that there would be liquidity at the end of the tunnel. The promise to drive the company to an IPO was actually a major negotiation point for Irving when discussing whether he would even take the CEO job, as it would be required to get the right people with the right backgrounds from the right companies to consider joining him at what was not considered at the time to even be a classically defined technology company.

Irving's tone in conveying his heroic credibility externally had less to do with pioneering a path for the industry and more to do with inclusion, with bringing everyone else along—particularly those who felt left out. "My philosophy for leading is get out in front, set the pace and live the culture you want everyone else to live," Irving said in a 2017 *Forbes* interview. "I often say lead from the front—but do it in the mosh pit, not on the stage."[1]

Today, GoDaddy is seen as a bellwether of inclusion and diversity, with a higher percentage of women in engineering roles than any of its Silicon Valley peers. The strategy has also coincided with an explosion of growth, as the formerly $1 billion brand has now surpassed $7 billion in revenue.

THE TRAPPINGS OF CULTURE

Before we leave the GoDaddy story, let's touch on one additional area of interest. Beyond the human interactions and perceptions, there is an equally important story to tell about the physical environment itself. One can't fully shift a culture if the environment doesn't match the words being said. And Irving was highly sensitive to the disconnect when he stepped into the role at GoDaddy.

"When I started at GoDaddy, they had never done anything to the facilities," Irving said. "It literally looked like an old retail storefront or an orthodontist's office. I told the board I'm going to spend money upgrading this. I can't bring guys here from Google or Microsoft and have them interview and take us seriously unless you feel like it's a tech company."

Irving set about building a campus that reflected the new image he and his team had worked so hard to establish. The new $27 million facility features a fitness area, a yoga room, a game center, an indoor climbing wall, a go-kart track, outdoor basketball and volleyball courts, and a soccer field. Not to mention the giant slide that sends employees down from the second floor to the area right outside the kitchen.

"We designed and built a facility in Tempe that became the number one facility in Arizona and it's just unbelievably cool," Irving said. "The new facility represents our culture. And then we repeated that everywhere else—we built in Seattle and the Bay Area, back East, and Europe now . . . you know, all of those things are physical manifestations of change. And every time somebody walks into work, they're reminded of this."

The physical, environmental side of culture change is an ever-present backdrop and reminder, as Irving says, that every time an employee walks into the building they are reminded of all the things that make up the brand. The color, the physical layout, the favorite amenities, even the humor of having a slide—all play roles in subtly influencing perceptions and behaviors that tell the viewer that yes, the culture isn't what it was when the previous regime was here . . . and the change wasn't just talk. The walls have literally moved. They're literally different colors now. And people throughout the community look at this new site and speak of it in a new tone of voice. All this matters.

In an age of increasingly distributed workforces, where employees might be down the hall or on the other side of the world, does this sort of thing still matter? Can culture change—or even survive—when employees aren't in the same place and interacting, on purpose and by accident, on a daily or at least frequent basis? Most companies today embrace remote work. But there's still a core of activity that surrounds the culture, there's still a feel to "headquarters" that carries meaning beyond the same company name we have on our LinkedIn profiles, if not business cards. We can attempt to re-create the accidental exposure we have to colleagues with video conferencing, but face-to-face isn't something that's easy to replicate with technology. Talking with a colleague on a video-conferencing system—even a great one, which is becoming the norm and not the exception—is not the same as sitting across a table face-to-face. This technological dislocation, where the human signal degrades over distance and bandwidth, is something that modern companies still need to deal with. Most do so by relying as best they can on technology—the entire economy of Unified Communications, video conferencing, and "work anywhere" is based on this—but the best ones create excuses to bring people together. They create forums for people to meet face-to-face and interact when they may not usually. And all of this relates to the physical space. We invest in headquarters and make it a place we're proud to work out of—or visit or bring customers to—because that's the physical root of culture, the shared feelings we have for the company whose mission we've all bought into—all summed up in a place.

As work is increasingly flung out from the traditional command and control environments of the past, we see greater emphasis on creating a place or a hub that we can all come home to and enjoy a sense of belonging and excitement. The investment in the HQ-plex is a critical part of culture and one many companies would do well to emulate.

KEY TAKEAWAYS

This in-depth exploration of cultural change represents yet another example of the power of how the three key elements—"seeking control in an out-of-control world," "raw," and "heroic credibility"—can work as a holistic system, a blueprint, to effect a behavior and values shift on an entire organization. Once we acknowledge that everyone in our company is, essentially, a person living in an age immersed totally in technology, where it impacts not only how we relate to the brands we buy or the candidates we support or the news we choose to believe in but also how we interact with our friends and anonymous contacts across the internet, we realize that this broad and deep cultural driver has affected all of our waking hours—including the hours we spend at work. The way a brand employs these tools to crack through the indifference of a distracted consumer market is not too different from how a new executive team might look to shift the perceptions and behaviors at work. Changing culture is a matter of changing behaviors, interactions, and expectations, first with individuals and later entire populations of workers. And when consumer sentiment suggests that we all desire to be treated a certain way and communicated with in a manner more suited to modern sensibilities, smart executives need to pay attention.

What are the big learnings we can take away from this discussion of culture change?

What systems can we put in place to ensure that we're always on when it comes to culture shift?

Changing a culture requires more than just an aspirational goal. It requires constant pressure. Think of the effect it would have had on the executive team at GoDaddy had Irving blown up at his new direct report or fired him on the spot for insubordination. This single act would have reversed everything the culture change had set out to do. The new managers would have felt betrayed, and the old ones would have felt vindicated for their reluctance to change their ways. The initiative would have died in the room.

Culture is an always-on pursuit. There are no days off, no casual slip-ups, and no exceptions. There will be designated cheerleaders, drivers, and mentors along the way. But the pressure needs to be constant and unwavering.

How many ways can we push trust to the top of the priority list when driving culture change?

Creating a bubble inside the company where new ways of behaving can be lived without judgment is critically important when everyone is worried about how they'll be accepted in a new culture. No one trusts the new guy. There are too many examples of new management coming on board and simply firing everybody to blindly trust what is going on. There is a natural reluctance to give up habits of the past, as well. In those cases where a "command and control" management style is being replaced by one more aptly described as "empower and align," we are usually starting out from a point of low trust. And trust must be fostered, slowly, before any real change can occur.

How much trust does the system have in the average worker on day one? How can a new executive push control of individual and group outcomes into the hands of the people who care about them the most? How much alignment can be achieved, how much evidence can be presented, how many times can the executive simply get out of the way and let the workforce see what they need to see so they can understand their likely outcomes without having to wonder in isolation where they stand?

How do we ensure we empower everyone—not just the big personalities—to act in the name of culture change?

There's probably a widely held misconception—and it's probably a Hollywood trope—that leaders need to be larger-than-life P. T.

Barnum–like characters who jump on tables and act in outlandish ways. Yes, there are plenty who do this, as we all know. But it's not the norm. Leadership—even the most inspirational leadership—comes from marshalling effort, harnessing passion, and bringing a company to a place that is more hopeful than where it is today. This effort doesn't always require being a larger-than-life showman. It simply requires connection. We all have different styles. Senior executives do, too. Some are soft-spoken, funny, introverted, fascinating people who are the antithesis of the Hollywood version. Some, on the other hand, are like Bob Parsons or Richard Branson or any other of the larger-than-life characters that we see quoted on a daily basis.

So we shouldn't feel that in order to lead a cultural change, outrageousness is required. We need the courage of our convictions, a clear sense of where we're starting from and where we're going, a workforce that is emboldened and empowered with trust and alignment, and the constant always-on attention to make sure it's being lived out, every day.

How can we ensure we're bringing in the right people and modeling the right behaviors at work?

You change a culture by hiring it. You hire people who embody the skills, mindset, and attitudes you want to see walking your halls every day. This doesn't mean you have to fire every legacy employee in the organization. But it does mean you need to shape the culture quickly by bringing in the sorts of people you need. Doing so serves two important roles. First, it creates an instant mini-culture within the organization of highly skilled and on-strategy people who can execute on day one the way you want things executed. Second, and perhaps more important in the long run, it provides an example for legacy employees for modeling their behavior. Those legacy employees who are successful at modeling this new way of doing things will survive and thrive. Those who can't, or decide that rebellion is the better course, will move on sooner or later. The choice in most cases is theirs.

What is the role of group identity, and how can we overcommunicate the definition of "we"?

The perception that management is above the fray, watching the workforce toil away in silent judgment, is going to stall growth. Aspiration requires that the leader leads the effort, and this is not something that can be delegated. Irving was clear when going through his alignment process with key managers that his role was to get the board to fund their ideas. This is a hugely important comment. Irving clearly articulated that his job was to remove obstacles and that he, too, had people watching him. This makes his role as the person asking the hard questions much easier for a skeptical audience to accept. We're all in this together, he says. "We" includes the CEO now. It isn't just "us" down here doing all the work and hoping the new guy on the top floor decides to approve it. If you want to lead, you have to be in the boat.

How can we ensure that technology helps, and doesn't damage, the culture?

The workforce is increasingly distributed, thanks to collaboration technology. Our colleagues, with whom we work on a daily basis, thanks to the miracle of videoconferencing and Unified Communications, might be downstairs, at the airport, or in their home office on the other side of the world. We can lean on this technology when we need it. But if it is the norm, rather than the exception, are we really part of a single culture?

Collaboration technology plays an interesting role in forging cultural bonds. It is always helpful to reframe the perception of video collaboration not as a poor substitute for a business trip but rather as something vastly superior to a voice call. Technology can help bridge distance and build relationships that would only have been possible to build face-to-face—and after a fairly long flight—a few short years ago. The real challenge within the scope of this cultural change conversation is to define the role collaboration technology can play to help build the bonds of the culture and not find ways for technology to allow it to slip away because of laziness or convenience. In other words, don't let the easy convenience of technology take the place of true cultural connection. Smart companies find ways to keep the core intact, in one location, so that culture can be fostered and grown by the accidental interactions between coworkers.

How can we elevate the role of the physical headquarters facility as a cultural symbol?

We also need to acknowledge the impact that the right environment has on our perceptions of culture. The physical space we work in sends a message and colors how we feel about the job we do. When we think about the benefits of investing in a physical headquarters space, we realize that it's the answer to the previous question surrounding the social dislocation of technology. If technology can't quite fill the gap left by people not all working in the same place all day long, perhaps the answer is creating a headquarters space that is something they're proud of and happy to visit, and then creating excuses to bring people together as often as is reasonable.

Some companies have no real headquarters. Other companies out there today rely on a workforce that is 100 percent remote. But they're rare. Companies that strive to have a cohesive culture forged with close relationships and great teamwork find ways to bring their people in. The physical side serves as a visual reminder of the culture.

How can we leverage "boring consistency"?

Have you ever heard of an *eigenvalue*? "This sentence has five words." That's an eigenvalue. Saying it defines it. This concept was pioneered by a scientist named Heinz von Foerster, known for his work forging a link between physics and philosophy and credited for being the father of cybernetics, a field that has impacted everything from cryptography to architecture to art; and this same self-defining principle applies to organizational culture change. Everything must be self-defining, from the interviews you give to the press, to the staff meetings and town halls you hold, to the facilities you renovate. Your brand needs to sing through the way your customer service and technical support teams answer the phone and the way your HR department handles on-boarding and termination. Everything needs to feel as though it could only come from you and that it could only embody the culture you seek to instill in the company. Anything that doesn't meet this criterion needs an overhaul.

When Irving discusses being "boringly consistent," this is what he's talking about.

What systems can we put in place to ensure that cultural change and buy-in happen at the individual level?

Cocreation creates joint ownership. When we're involved in the process or when we actually own the process, we're automatically bought in. This goes for product development as much as it does for cultural change. Irving's many examples of assigning owners and having them—not him—come up with decision criteria, milestones, budgets, and all of the operational aspects of the part of the whole that they owned give us a good idea of how to ensure there's no indifference or pushback. We don't rebel when it's our plan.

Look back at the eigenvalue idea and apply this concept. If everything we, as a company, do must be self-defining and represent the brand and culture we desire, then it stands to reason we should describe the goal and the direction and then have the respective owners develop the operational plans to get us where we need to go for their specific areas of expertise. This is a very powerful exercise to run with your team. You'd be surprised to hear what a part of the organization you might not instantly associate with outbound communication or the visible bits of the culture can come up with, because they're often the most interested in engaging in this process precisely because they have traditionally felt like outsiders. Conversely, you may also find that those parts of the organization you feel would take to a cultural change initiative the most are the most resistant to change. After all, they're the most entrenched in the outward manifestations of the old way of doing things. Your results may vary, of course, so it's important to view this as a process and not a series of expectations.

What processes can we put in place to ensure aspirational goals are aligned with individual expectations?

Everything is politics. Everything is social. You can't separate the outside world of media, controversy, or sentiment from the inside world of the company and its nascent culture. It is therefore of paramount importance that we understand the values of the team before we set out to change their behaviors. This is nowhere more evident than in Silicon Valley, where GoDaddy's stance on SOPA created tension within the ranks. In this case, the legislation died in committee, and thus, the previous management team's opinions on it became moot, but the point is still important to consider. What are the prevailing sentiments and values of the team—both legacy and new hires—and how will any specific element of the cultural shift affect them?

We need to run through a checklist to ensure we've poked into all the right places when dealing with an issue this sticky. If we're going to pursue a global agenda and be citizens of the world, planting design centers in far-flung locations and tapping into a worldwide talent pool (all admirable things), what happens when we experience geopolitical instability? What happens when the country within which we've just hired a hundred designers—or a thousand software engineers—does something our workforce doesn't like or that our customers don't like? Do we say something—and if so, what do we say? Or are we quiet?

How would an economic downturn affect our efforts and being closer to communities where we may not have a clearly visible return on investment? Do we stay or do we shut down the initiative? Where does our team stand on issues like these, and are they going to be consistent with where we end up?

It's going to be critical to understand the extended team's values before planting a flag and trying to rally them to a cause that you hope they believe in. There's a lot to discuss when you have the chance to hold those town halls, but skipping over the bigger issues in favor of small talk is dangerous.

CONCLUSION

"It's not like there's a seminal moment when you say, 'OK! The culture's changed!' . . . it's an everyday thing, you have to live it every day," Irving relates. "And you can't just tell people what to do, you have to represent it."

Living it every day is perhaps the reality of a great cultural undertaking. Once the big ideas are white boarded and the tasks assigned and progress has taken root, what happens next? And what happens next week and next month? The answer is that we keep going. We live the culture out, and it impacts our work and our lives outside work. And this is hard.

"The unfortunate thing for me and why I burned out after five years was because Bob was such a big personality," Irving said. "To drive the company quickly, I had to have a big personality as well. It just had to be very, very different. And so I felt like a lot of times I was doing stuff that was outrageous, like dressing in orange pants or bright green pants, or wearing shorts and flip flops or doing things that were just different and being wide open."

When we're viewing a culture change initiative, it's perhaps oversimplistic to only look forward to the big ideas to come. Any change initiative needs to clearly comprehend the past. And the shoes Irving had to fill at GoDaddy were big. Founder Bob Parsons was a larger-than-life entrepreneur who forged its initial culture in his own image. He was mercurial, forceful, and incredibly bold in his approach; he was also incredibly generous with his time and money and a wonderfully warm and loyal person. Stepping on stage after his exit was, no doubt, an extraordinarily hard act to follow. And it required constant pressure and presence. But over time, once the new culture was no longer so new, it needed less course correction. At this point, Irving—having accomplished the Herculean task of shifting GoDaddy's culture 180 degrees—felt comfortable stepping away and handing the position to the next CEO of the company.

PART 4

The Future

Where do we go from here?

If, in our pursuit of a more unfiltered approach to marketing, we fully embrace the idea that raw is an emergent trend, how do we see the future unfolding? Is this phenomenon here to stay? Will it continue on its present course and become something more evolved? Or will we see a retrenchment and a reversal to more traditional expectations?

Over the past several years of studying these macro trends, we've seen substantial evidence to support the longevity of these big ideas. We see continuing evidence that seeking control in an out-of-control world continues to be a defining theme of current culture, particularly when we look at sentiment regarding digital security, personal privacy, and the definition of success centered on control over outcomes and personal time. We see evidence that raw is a continuing trend, albeit with a number of subtle shifts over time: where once rawness was synonymous with selfie-view video on all social platforms, we see a strong sense of fatigue behind this instance, likely due to overuse. We see a resurgence of sentiment in favor of ensuring we "have the facts" before speculating. But as for getting information directly from the source, the trend is still solid. When we look at heroic credibility, we see values alignment going through a wild shift—tremendous support for political and social justice collapsed in late 2018, signaling the death of outrage and a strong desire for credibility instead of strident lecturing.

Given all of this—and the syntheses that spring from these insights—we have a substantial and well-supported framework for guiding stewards of business today and in the immediate future. But what comes after that? Can we look into the next few years beyond our immediate time frame and feel our way toward a likely future state—or a small number of likely future states?

CHAPTER 11

Three Scenarios for the Future

It has been said, in various forms by various clever people, that plotting the future is akin to setting a future date at which even the most ignorant fool can mock you with impunity. And yet, if we're to put forward a current theory of the intersection of technology and culture that can help brands and others better communicate and persuade today, the very least we can do is to give the "fools of the future" the ammunition they'll need to mock us in a few years—before any of us have reason to suspect that we were off track at all. So, with some sense of bravery and no small portion of heroic credibility, let us put forward a few plausible scenarios for the future.

THE DIFFERENCE BETWEEN SCENARIO PLANNING AND FORTUNE TELLING

Before we step off into the slightly unknown, a word of caution— and explanation: what we're doing here is a quick exercise in scenario planning. This means we're looking at unarguable trends and combining them with our own insight, judgment, and no small bit of storytelling to create a few different narratives that can animate one or more plausible future states.

None are necessarily to be taken as gospel truth. The best way to interpret each is to look at it in two dimensions. Each scenario can be viewed as having a certain likelihood of coming true. Each, as well, can be viewed as having a certain maturity. We may choose to look at Scenario 1 as having a 75 percent chance of coming true but only a likelihood of 25 percent that it will come true the way we've described it in the time period we're studying. Not all of the more future-looking scenarios will unfold as quickly as we've described them. Some will happen faster than anticipated. Your results may vary depending on key political, industry, and social figures making unpredictable decisions that have ripple effects across all of society.

But the importance of this exercise can't be understated. Only by exploring where we're likely to go next can we better poke and prod into the appropriate corners to flesh out contingency plans, float new pilot programs, or discover new opportunities that can either head off future problems or proactively create a future state that stacks the cards in your favor. We need to have an idea of what the future might look like—for better or worse—before we can identify the triggers that indicate one scenario or another is suddenly emerging from the pack.

WHAT IS THE FUTURE GOING TO LOOK LIKE?

We don't see things as staying the same. We do see the culture moving in one of three potential directions. Here's how things might play out.

SCENARIO 1: TRIBAL NATION

What's the headline today?

> "Continued political bombast from both parties turns instant media access into a mud-slinging contest, with viewers on traditional, digital, and social channels largely tuning out—and tuning in to their own team's communications at the expense of any other viewpoint."

Socially, in this tribal nation world, we turn inward, toward our own tribes, communities, and families, with media consumption habits largely swinging like a pendulum back toward those we consider authorities and those select citizen-journalist types who have separated themselves from the pack, approaching levels of authority and followership that have traditionally been reserved for credentialed members of the media, while lesser-known figures fade. There are the beginnings of a backlash against the "chaos of choice."

Culturally, we've split into our respective camps and stick to our own tribes—in real life where possible and always online. We now have our brands, our restaurants, our venture capital firms, our networks, our movie and music stars, even our energy sources. Where once it would have seemed strange for a brand to emerge that caters specifically to one or another tribe, now this is fairly normal.

How do we view our key macro trends as they mature over this period of time?

Seeking control in an out-of-control world and the desire for personal control and sustainable living go up, with a deep hunger for self-sufficiency and a subtle nod toward learning to live without members of the other tribe underpinning our actions.

The hunger for raw is tempered by downward pressures on wide-open social platforms as the rise of curation drives a taste for more polished and professional presentation. Raw as a concept is more mainstreamed than it is today, but its focus is on context around "our" values and cocreation with "our" people. Unscripted is perhaps less important, as our levels of trust in "our" tribe are higher, while we simply don't engage much with "their" opinions.

Heroic credibility moves strongly in the direction of values alignment, with outrage focused on the "other" team.

What's the definition of community in this scenario? Community means "the people like me who think like me and are in and on my feed."

What's a Brand to Do in an Environment of Tribal Nation?

In this scenario, brands need to make a choice: either tread the very fine line of finding ways to appeal broadly—without throwing support heavily to one side or another—or go all-in on picking a tribe.

Can brands find a higher point on the pyramid and create a position that can be translated to multiple camps without alienating any? This will become harder and harder to manage, particularly over longer periods of time, where the outrage mob still exists. For those unwilling to take on this daunting assignment, or for those who are firebrands themselves, there's always the option of picking a side.

Communication and brand narratives need to be available on a wider number of discrete platforms, with messaging geared subtly (or not) to specific groups. Cocreation, likewise, needs to focus on developing products and services for specific subgroups, each with differing needs and behaviors. Speaking the language of the market—"swimming in the culture"—may never have been as important as it is now in this new world, with fluent and unscripted presentation geared toward a trusting audience willing to believe those it considers to be "one of us." In this new tribal setting, context must be couched in specific terms and considering very particular belief systems.

This scenario has serious implications for corporate culture and leadership styles. How can we, as leaders attempting to shape a workplace culture, ensure that everyone feels a part of the same team—at least at work?

SCENARIO 2: MAINSTREAMING PRIVACY

What's the headline today?

"Major social media platforms have been declared common carriers, ending fears of de-platforming and bias. Twitter, Facebook, and others become extensions of 'the news.' And while DNA capturing ancestry hobby services unwittingly provide the raw material to solve decades-old cold murder cases, there is a growing body of evidence gaining a wider audience that smart devices, from home appliances to wearables, are being hacked for nefarious purposes. As a result, more and more people are turning to a new option—a newer definition of 'social,' where they can best control security and privacy and a tighter, more secure definition of 'personal.' We still curate content these days. But now, we also look to curate the people with whom we share our content."

Suddenly, social is no longer cool. It's not just about curation of the chaotic flow of raw information swirling around us, but the curation of people in our network. When social platforms become just another part of the news media institution, the cool kids look to create and maintain something of their own—their own private encrypted options. We communicate within our own private groups, discussing things we feel are private, and do so with heavy encryption. Even calls to grandma are encrypted now.

Culturally, there's less tribal behavior than in retrenchment, but more of a small circle of friends and other like-minded people. We still get our news online from "official" sources, but the discussion and opinion creation happen away from prying eyes.

Seeking control in an out-of-control world continues to dominate our personal lives, with a greater sense of privacy and security emerging as our top priorities—our way of regaining control is by encrypting it. We are increasingly aware of who makes our platforms, where they are hosted, and what agendas each has in the greater scheme of things. The public, in large part, still distrusts what's around them.

Raw steadily increases as a social and professional expectation, given the mainstreaming of capture and dissemination platforms, along with a growing population of contextual streamers from all walks of life continuing to flow into the online world.

Heroic credibility—from bold messaging and values alignment to brand advocacy—becomes more important than ever as the noise level continues to increase. As values are shared and opinions honed in tightly controlled groups, reaching these tight-knit communities is a matter of meeting them where they are—in the real world and online, in as many relevant media choices as possible.

Politicians, community leaders, brands, and others mainstream the instant access and first-person perspective with in-context video, as app providers make voice-over and other contextual editing easier for the everyday user in real time. Smart home providers, seeing the writing on the wall, invest heavily in data security and beef up their efforts to ensure devices are anonymized and data isn't captured, creating entire departments of quasi-political-security officers in anticipation of a greater governmental crackdown, which doesn't come.

Community means "those people in my personal encrypted circle."

What's a Brand to Do in an Environment of Mainstreaming Privacy?

In this scenario, trust is thrust to the fore. Going above and beyond current definitions of data sovereignty and data security will be a mandatory means of staying current in the cultural conversation. Investing in the technology necessary to lock down digital security and hacker-proofing devices, appliances, and applications all become mandatory. Equally important is how this is all communicated to a skeptical buying public that wants to see the proof and understand how you're going to ensure, over time, that their information is safe with you.

Where once "speaking the language of the market" was a function of understanding big, widely spoken vocabularies, now it's akin to speaking a hundred different dialects, each with certain subtleties and nuances. It will be impossible to speak them all without recruiting a legion of interpreters, and the only way to do that is to create experts, win over skeptics, and build an unassailable surplus of trust.

SCENARIO 3: ME-STREAM

What's the headline today?

"The maverick president of the United States decides to wear a livestreaming body camera twelve hours a day, narrating many of his meetings and calls in real time, half to his attendees and half to his online audience of billions. There is literally too much information to synthesize, as battalions of foreign intelligence operatives, attempting to gain insight from this unending torrent of information, collapse in exhaustion—there's no time to synthesize or make sense of what's being said because it never stops. When the vice president, half of the members of Congress, and the first several thousand key members of the business community follow suit, it results in a revolution in personal media."

The social impact of "Me-Stream" is that everyone aspires to be one of the few that the rest watch; the influencer model is elevated to a level that's hard to imagine today. We all want to be someone whose life is worth livestreaming. But in this new world, where everyone is a broadcaster, is anyone a reader or listener? Attention spans noticeably shrink, sound bites replace full sentences, and no one has time to read a full tweet.

It's hard to keep up, so we can't—but we try. Speed replaces completion. Advertising units are now developed for parts of a second. With the pyramid becoming a needle, the digital and economic divide becomes stark. Digital security and personal security become significant concerns to those who can afford them. The need to seek control of a life fully out of technological control becomes a two-headed monster; the convenience and psychological pull of greater technological advances are enticing, but the loss of privacy is a real issue.

Seeking control in an out-of-control world splits into two subtrends, where frictionless convenience and entertainment come with a significant loss of privacy, while security for personal data becomes mandatory.

Raw explodes beyond its current boundaries as booming populations are streaming—or attempting to stream—every facet of their lives.

Heroic credibility in terms of brand alignment and bold messaging increase to a fevered pitch as the war for attention shifts into an exponentially higher orbit. There is so much noise and so much frequency that it's hard to focus. No one has time for boycotts anymore.

Technology focuses on the immensely expanded role of video. But with everything focused on livestreaming, there's a countervailing trend: the offline world and the concept of face-to-face become the revolutionary way to interact and engage.

What's the definition of community? Community means "the people who follow me."

What's a Brand to Do in an Environment of Me-Stream?

Brands have to balance the immediacy and frenetic pace of stream wars with the countervailing trend of offline, experiential marketing. In some cases, this may mean they need to make serious choices. The culture is streaming everything; so brands, if they want to be part of this cultural conversation, will need to participate. On the other hand, the counterculture is rejecting this always-on immediacy and creating a new "slow food" movement of its own, connecting with other people in a human, offline world.

Think of what this scenario means for leaders: balancing the needs of the company with the needs of the workers, many of whom are brands themselves at this point. What happens when you have a department of a hundred you need to manage and five of them are livestreaming meetings, decisions, designs, thought processes, and trade secrets that your legal team says are too sensitive to say out loud? How do you give personal brands the room to be evangelists but also the constraints to work effectively with others?

THE MULTIVERSE OF SCENARIOS

These are three scenarios. If you spend time with any trend framework—ours, yours, or anyone else's, not to mention all of them together—you, too, can author a series of great scenarios that can speak to your specific sensitivities. We picked these three because they offer themselves up as good, vivid caricatures of where we might be going next. One animates the growing divide and how to navigate a world of increasing division and polarization. We see strong evidence today of "our" brands versus "their" brands across the spectrum of industries. The next delves into deeper, darker digital security and the fear of a world undone by hackers. This is not a stretch. And last, a world where the influencer and livestreaming model goes atomic is not hard to see coming.

Will any of these happen the way we've described here? We don't need to predict whether the answer is "yes" or "no" at the moment; we just need to understand what each means to our business, from the likely triggers that suggest one or another is about to burst on the scene to the contingency plans, opportunity planning, and pilot program development that can turn any of them to your advantage.

So, don't take this discussion too literally. Squint and find the kernel of truth in it. Understand why it's here. Plan accordingly.

CONCLUSION

Where we fall within this—or any—group of scenarios is up for debate and very much subject to butterfly effect–like forces happening in the next twelve months, from political to economic, social, cultural, environmental, and technological forces.

What isn't up for debate is this: technology has emerged as the single most profound cultural driver in the world today, shaping how we interact with the brands we buy, how we manage our digital footprints, and how we approach an increasingly distributed workplace. And this profound impact will not lessen over the next generation.

We are social creatures, and technology has emerged as a symbiotic force in our lives, causing significant changes in our brain function and physical constitution. We often see technology ultimately used in a fashion at odds with its original intent; and this accidental mutation, in turn, occasionally changes us as well.

The key lesson of this book is how we can take advantage of macro waves to accomplish our aims, be they in fields of business, politics, philanthropy, or simply interpersonal influence. Use this book as a blueprint or a playbook. Incorporate these ideas into your operating plans, communication platforms, sales strategies, or new product development road maps.

The purpose of this work is to exhort the reader to greater success in life. In this, we wish you the best of luck!

CHAPTER NOTES

INTRODUCTION

1. Christopher Vollmer and Daniel Gross, "NBA Commissioner Adam Silver Has a Game Plan," *strategy + business*, April 30, 2018, *www.strategy-business .com*.

2. Kelly McLaughlin, "The Man Who Taught Donald Trump How to Tweet Likens Him to Velociraptors Learning to Open Doors in 'Jurassic Park,'" *Business Insider—South Africa*, December 23, 2018, *www.businessinsider.co.za*.

CHAPTER 1

1. "Edelman Trust Barometer 2017," Edelman, accessed November 15, 2019, *www.edelman.com*.

2. "[Fixed Issue] Google Home Mini Touch Controls Behaving Incorrectly," Google Nest Help, Google, accessed November 15, 2019, *support.google.com*.

3. David Goldman, "Your Samsung TV Is Eavesdropping on Your Private Conversations," *CNNMoney*, Cable News Network, February 10, 2015, *money .cnn.com*.

4. "Demographics of Mobile Device Ownership and Adoption in the United States," Pew Research Center: Internet, Science & Tech, June 12, 2019, *www .pewresearch.org*.

5. "Demographics of Internet and Home Broadband Usage in the United States."

6. Andrew Perrin and Monica Anderson, "Share of U.S. Adults Using Social Media, Including Facebook, Is Mostly Unchanged since 2018," Pew Research Center, April 10, 2019, *www.pewresearch.org*.

7. "Monthly Comparisons of Internet Speeds from around the World," Speedtest Global Index, accessed November 15, 2019, *www.speedtest.net*.

CHAPTER 2

1. George Selfo, "Q&AA: T-Mobile CEO John Legere Loves to Be Hated," *Ad Age*, March 13, 2018.

2. Amy Chozick, "With 'Talking to Strangers,' Malcolm Gladwell Goes Dark," *New York Times*, August 30, 2019.

3. Oprah Winfrey, "What Oprah Knows for Sure about Authenticity," accessed March 10, 2020, *www.oprah.com*.

4. Herminia Ibarra, "The Authenticity Paradox," *Harvard Business Review*, January–February, 2015.

5. Ibid.

6. Asad Meah, "40 Inspirational Anna Wintour Quotes on Success," accessed May 7, 2019, *www.awakenthegreatnesswithin.com*.

7. Margaret Lyons, "On 'Couples Therapy,' Domestic Angst Is Raw and Delicious," *New York Times*, September 5, 2019.

8. Walter Isaacson, *Steve Jobs* (New York: Simon & Schuster, 2011), 565.

9. Paul Leinberger, personal communication, October 1986.

10. Steve Jobs, "You've Got to Find What You Love, Jobs Says," *Stanford News*, June 14, 2005.

11. Meah, "40 Inspirational Anna Wintour Quotes."

12. Ibid.

13. Mike Robbins, "Mike Robbins—Authenticity in the Workplace," filmed August 8, 2017, YouTube video, 32:19 min., *www.youtube.com*.

14. Daniel Zhang and Daniel Zipser, "Speak Softly, Make Tough Decisions: An Interview with Alibaba Group Chairman and CEO Daniel Zhang," *McKinsey Quarterly*, September 2019, *www.mckinsey.com*.

15. Emma London, "5 CEOs Who Are Doing Social Media Right," *CEOWorld Magazine*, November 13, 2018.

16. Cisco Visual Networking Index: Forecast and Trends, 2017–2022 White Paper. Updated February 27, 2019.

17. Adam Hayes, "The State of Video Marketing in 2019," Hubspot Marketing, 2019, *blog.hubspot.com*.

18. Caroline Golum, "The Future of Live Video: 26 Influencers Share Their Thoughts," Livesteam, 2017, *livestream.com*.

19. Kathy Klotz, "The Best Brand Experiments with Live Streaming Video," Convince&Convert, 2017, *www.convinceandconvert.com*.

20. Rod Griffin, "How Social Media Is Changing Financial Literacy," Equities.com, April 28, 2016, *www.equities.com*.

21. Bernard Marr, "How Experian Is Using Big Data and Machine Learning to Cut Mortgage Application Times to a Few Days," *Forbes*, May 25, 2017, *www.forbes.com*.

22. GM Corporate Newsroom, "Mid-Engine Chevrolet Corvette Reveal to Be Livestreamed Globally," July 8, 2019, *www.forbes.com*.

23. Chris Bruce, "2020 Chevy Corvette Stingray Nearly Sold Out for First Model Year," Motor1.com, July 29, 2019, *www.motor1.com*.

24. Alexandra Steigrad, "Food Network to Launch App That Streams Interactive Cooking Classes," *New York Post*, September 25, 2019, *nypost.com*.

25. "Meet Vimeo Enterprise: Video for the Way You Work," Vimeo Livestream, *livestream.com*.

26. Golum, "The Future of Live Video."

CHAPTER 3

1. Cara Salpini, "Glossier Raises $100M in Latest Funding Round," Retail Dive, March 20, 2019, *www.retaildive.com*.

2. Jon Bird, "How Glossier Turned a Blog into a Billion-Dollar Brand," *Forbes*, March 25, 2019, *www.forbes.com*.

3. Nitasha Tiku, "Inside Glossier, the Beauty Startup That Reached Cult Status by Selling Less," *BuzzFeed News*, August 25, 2016, *www.buzzfeednews.com*.

CHAPTER 4

1. Todd Bishop and Taylor Soper, "Future of Sports Viewing? Steve Ballmer and L.A. Clippers Debut New Augmented Reality NBA Experience," *GeekWire*, October 19, 2018, *www.geekwire.com*.

2. Aaron Falk, "NBA Commissioner Adam Silver Discusses Fan Experience, 5 for the Fight Patch at Qualtrics Summit," NBA.com—Utah Jazz, March 7, 2019, *www.nba.com*.

3. "How Do Adam Silver and Roger Goodell View Influence of Tech?," *Front Office Sports*, July 16, 2019, *frontofficesport.com*.

4. Kindra Cooper, "NBA Redesigns Fan Experience for the Social Media Generation," *CCW Digital | Customer Experience Tips, Research & News*, March 26, 2019, *www.customercontactweekdigital.com*.

CHAPTER 5

1. Andrew Caesar, "Dumping Reputation in Pursuit of Sales," *PRWeek*, October 28, 2015.

2. Ibid.

3. Rich Duprey, "Dick's Sporting Goods Still Feeling Impact of Its Gun Ban," *Motley Fool*, April 13, 2019.

4. Paul Watson, "Gillette Sales Decline Following 'Toxic Masculinity' Ad," *Summit News*, April 26, 2019, *https://summit.news*

5. Jack Neff, "Gillette's 'The Best Men Can Be' and the War on Toxic Masculinity," *Ad Age*, September 30, 2019, 24.

6. Ibid.

7. Justin Fox, "The Social Responsibility of Business Is to Increase . . . What Exactly?," *Harvard Business Review*, April 18, 2012.

8. David Gelles and David Yaffe-Bellany, "Shareholder Value Is No Longer Everything, Top C.E.O.s Say," *New York Times*, August 19, 2019.

9. Elizabeth Dilts, "Top U.S. CEOs Say Companies Should Put Social Responsibility above Profit," *Reuters*, August 19, 2019.

10. Editorial Board, "The 'Stakeholder' CEOs." *Wall Street Journal*, August 19, 2019, *www.wsj.com*.

11. Gelles and Yaffe-Bellany, "Shareholder Value Is No Longer Everything."

12. Alan Murray, "A New Purpose for the Corporation," *Fortune*, September 2019, 88.

13. Ibid.

14. Editorial Board, "What Are Companies For?," *Economist*, August 24, 2019, 7.

15. Murray, "A New Purpose for the Corporation," 92.

16. Simon Sinek, *Start with Why* (New York: The Penguin Group, 2009).

17. Businesswire, "Levi Strauss & Co. Announces Fourth Quarter & Fiscal Year 2018 Financial Results," February 5, 2019.

18. Levi Strauss & Co., "Guided by Principles and Inspired to Innovate," accessed September 4, 2019, *www.levistrauss.com*.

19. Ibid.

20. Levi Strauss & Co., "We Believe . . . Giving Back Never Goes Out of Style," accessed September 5, 2019, *www.levistrauss.com*.

21. Kate Bravery, "People First: Mercer's 2018 Global Talent Trends Study," *Mercer*, May 28, 2018.

22. Alan Kohll, "What Employees Really Want at Work," *Forbes*, July 10, 2018, *www.forbes.com*.

23. Bravery, "People First."

24. Harvard Business School's Project on Managing the Future of Work and BCG's Henderson Institute, "The Future of Human Work Workers Survey," 2018, *www.hbs.edu*.

25. Deloitte, "The Deloitte Global Millennial Survey 2018," accessed March 10, 2020, *www2.deloitte.com*.

26. Deloitte, "The Deloitte Global Millennial Survey 2019," accessed March 10, 2020, *www2.deloitte.com*.

27. Andrew Winston, "Is the Business Roundtable Statement Just Empty Rhetoric?," *HBR* podcast, August 30, 2019.

28. MarketWatch, "Unilever Trumps U.S. Rivals with Solid Sales," February 1, 2018, *www.marketwatch.com*.

29. Levi Strauss & Co., "Guided by Principles."

CHAPTER 6

1. Kate Taylor, "The Retail Apocalypse Is Far from Over as Analysts Predict 75,000 More Store Closures," *Business Insider,* April 9, 2019.

2. Monica Anderson, "Mobile Technology and Home Broadband 2019," Pew Research Center, June 13, 2019.

3. Nicole Fisher, "How Much Time Americans Spend in Front of Screens Will Terrify You," *Forbes*, January 24, 2019.

4. Peter Kim, "The Fusion of Creative, Media and Technology," MightyHive website, May 14, 2019.

5. Blake Morgan, "50 Retail Innovation Stats That Prove the Power of Customer Experience," *Forbes*, May 21, 2019.

6. Michelle Beeson, "Retailers Are Starting to Reap the Rewards of Omnichannel Commerce," *Forrester Report*, April 29, 2019.

7. Nicolas Maechler, Kevin Neher, and Rober Park, "From Touchpoints to Journeys: Seeing the World as Customers Do," *McKinsey Insights*, March 2016.

8. Ibid.

9. Ibid.

CHAPTER 7

1. Richard Trenholm, "'Unsane' Shows Anyone Can Make an Average Film on an iPhone," *CNET*, March 29, 2018, *www.cnet.com*.

2. Eric Kohn, "Steven Soderbergh Says He's Done Directing Studio Movies and Wants to Only Shoot on iPhones—Sundance 2018," *IndieWire*, January 27, 2018, *www.indiewire.com*.

3. Stephen Denny, "Note to CMO: Storytelling, Persuasion, and Death by PowerPoint," StephenDenny.com, December 30, 2009, *www.stephendenny.com*.

CHAPTER 8

1. Kyt Dotson, "Delta Air Lines Flight Cancellations Possibly Caused by Data Center Fire," *SiliconAngle*, August 6, 2016.

2. Ibid. (Original Twitter feed no longer available.)

3. "Q&A with Ed Bastian, 2017 Most Admired CEO," *Atlanta Business Chronicle*, July 31, 2017.

4. Richard Feloni, "The T-Mobile CEO Who Called His Competition 'Dumb and Dumber' Explains How He Doubled Customers in 4 Years, and How a Group of Employees Made Him Cry," *Business Insider*, October 7, 2016.

5. SC Johnson, *2016 Sustainability Report*, 2016, 36, *www.scjohnson.com*.

6. Fisk Johnson, "SC Johnson's CEO on Doing the Right Thing, Even When It Hurts Business," *Harvard Business Review*, April 2015, 33–36.

7. Fisk Johnson, "Earning Good Will in a Crisis of Consumer Trust" (speech, presented at Ratheon Lectureship in Business Ethics, Bentley University, October 2, 2017).

8. SC Johnson, "A Company Values Speech That Changed SC Johnson Forever: The Rest Is Shadow," accessed March 10, 2020, *www.scjohnson.com*.

9. SC Johnson website, *www.scjohnson.com*.

10. Ibid.

11. SC Johnson, *2019 Sustainability Report*, 2019, 2, *www.scjohnson.com*.

12. Johnson, "Earning Good Will."

13. SC Johnson, *2018 Sustainability Report*, 2018, 1, *www.scjohnson.com*.

14. Ibid, 2.

15. Dale Buss, "SC Johnson Chief Fisk Johnson Dives Deep, Goes Wide Against Plastic Wastes," *Chief Executive*, April 11, 2019.

16. SC Johnson, *2019 Sustainability Report*, 2–3.

17. Amy Anderson, "How Delta CEO Ed Bastian Just Proved That Delta Airlines Cares," *Forbes*, October 19, 2016.

18. David Sloan, "High Flyer Interview: Delta's Ed-Volution According to Ed Bastian," *Always Magazine*, August 6, 2019.

19. David Giles, "Leadership Is Not a Popularity Contest," *New York Times*, February 21, 2019.

20. Ibid.

21. Ibid.

22. Ibid.

23. Fortune Editors, "The World's Greatest Leaders," *Fortune*, April 19, 2018

CHAPTER 9

1. "Is Activism Good Business? A Conversation with Patagonia's CEO," YouTube, June 27, 2018, 53.29 min., *www.youtube.com*.

2. Patagonia, "Inside Patagonia," accessed on July 12, 2018, *www.patagonia.com*.

3. Ibid., accessed on November 11, 2019, *www.patagonia.com*.

4. Ibid., accessed on December 3, 2019, *www.patagonia.com*

5. Yvon Chouinard, "A Consumer Revolution," *Orion Magazine*, March 3, 2014.

6. Jeff Beer, "Uphill Climb," *Fast Company*, November 2019.

7. Digital Transformation Institute, "Fixing the Cracks: Reinventing Loyalty Programs for the Digital Age," Capgemini, 2015.

8. Colloquy Customer Loyalty Census, 2017.

9. "From Transient to Resolute: How Deep Does Loyalty Go?," Maritz Motivation Solutions, 2018, *www.prweb.com.*

10. Capgemini Digital Transformation Institute study, "The Key to Loyalty," August–September 2017.

11. Ibid.

12. Jim Greulich and Jennifer Buchanan, "Driving Brand Loyalty with Emotion," *Deloitte Digital*, May 23, 2019.

13. Jeff Neff, "Innovation Intervention," *Ad Age*, November 18, 2019, 21.

14. Ibid., 18.

CHAPTER 10

1. Zack Friedman, "GoDaddy CEO Blake Irving on How to Be a Boss," *Forbes*, July 13, 2017, *www.forbes.com.*

INDEX

cultural change (*continued*)
  at individual level, 208–209
  new hires and, 205–206
  overview of, 191–192
  physical environment and,
    200–202
  raw and, 196–198
  self-defining principle and,
    207–208
  systems to aid in, 203–204
  technology and, 206–207
  trust and, 204
culture
  adidas and, 53
  business world and, 6–7
  C2B, creating, 127–129
  cocreation and, 58
  contact and, 57–58
  entertainment and, 4–6
  immersed in technology, being
    unscripted against, 41–43
  in-process as immersion in,
    56–57, 68–69
  Live PD impact on, 74, 77
  news media and, 1–4
  Pentagon Papers and, 17
  technology and, 1–11 (*See also*
    consumer-to-business (C2B)
    economy)
Culture & Technology Intersection
  study, 13
Curtis, Susanna, 166
customer loyalty, 183–186
cybernetics, 208

data
  actively collected, 22–23
  consumer-to-business (C2B),
    129–131
  in-context theme, 87, 88

in-process theme, 65–67
internet access, 27–28
livestreaming, 49
passively collected, 23
smartphone, 27–28
social media usage, 27–28
storytelling, 148–151
trust, 21–24
De Laurentiis, Giada, 46
Deloitte Global, 47
Deloitte Millennial survey, 102–103
Delta Airlines, 157–158
  brand militancy and, 168–169
  heroic credibility at, 168–169
  leadership blueprint at, 165–171,
    176, 180
  raw use at, 167–168
  seeking control at, 165–167
democratization of technology,
  26–29
Denny Leinberger Strategy, 7
DICK's Sporting Goods, 94, 104
digital marketing environment, C2B
  economy and, 117–120
Dimon, Jamie, 96
direct access, 54
"disarm and assail" playbook,
  193–196
disconnect, unscripted approach to
  leadership and, 36
Discovery, Inc., 47
distraction, technology and, 84–85
Dumbo (movie), 141–142

Echo speaker, 18
Economist, 96, 97
ecosystem, in-process as, 58–61
eigenvalue, 207–208
Ellsberg, Daniel, 15–16, 26–27
empathy, 100

About the Authors

Paul Leinberger is a bestselling author, speaker, and consultant helping companies craft market-leading brand strategies, develop competitive positioning, and understand the impact of changing consumer trends. He is the coauthor of the international bestseller *The New Individualists*. The roster of companies Paul has consulted for includes Microsoft, Sony, Cisco, Starbucks, General Mills, Nestlé, SC Johnson, Kimberly-Clark, Nordstrom, and Disney. Paul holds a PhD in organizational and social psychology and a Master of Urban Planning. He lives in Irvine, California.

Stephen Denny is an author, speaker, and consultant, helping emerging and well-established brands define (or redefine) their competitive positioning. He is the author of *Killing Giants*. The roster of companies Stephen has consulted for and spoken to ranges from start-ups to Global 500 players, including Logitech, The North Face, Altria, Hewlett-Packard, Elsevier, Campbell's Soup Company, and others. Prior to consulting, Steve held the senior marketing executive position at several companies: Plantronics, Sony, OnStar (General Motors), and Iomega, over a twenty-plus–year period. Stephen has lived and worked in both the United States and Japan, has an MBA from the Wharton School of the University of Pennsylvania, and lives near Denver, Colorado.

ABOUT DENNY LEINBERGER STRATEGY

Denny Leinberger Strategy is a boutique consultancy focused on spotting the trends that drive business performance and then giving our clients the tools and insights to act on them so they can achieve real-world financial results.

We first launched the Culture & Technology Intersection study in 2016 and have been exploring the implications for clients ever since. For brands struggling with how to take advantage of this cultural shift—from the development of a "digital strategy" to the needs of the "always-on" consumer to the implications of the virtual workplace—the Culture & Technology Intersection study provides both the data and the insight to help drive bottom-line results.

The American Mindset is a large-scale segmentation study that involves understanding the attitudes of the American public in six different areas, providing insights at the MSA level.

If you're interested in cosponsoring either of these important studies, please reach out to us.

Denny Leinberger Strategy is also happy to provide additional consulting services, as follows:

Keynote Speeches: Both agency principals are available to keynote sales meetings, executive retreats, key customer strategic reviews, or other events where bigger picture concepts would help elevate the conversation and stimulate big ideas.

Scenario Planning: We offer a multiday workshop devoted to planning different potential future scenarios to allow decisions makers to better understand how the future is likely to unfold. This is particularly useful to senior management, strategic planning, and line management for strategic investments and budget planning over a five-year time horizon.

Strategic Planning: We offer consulting services that add on to scenario planning to ensure that strategies are aligned with potential outcomes, client culture, and capabilities. As former line managers ourselves, we're in a unique position to guide strategy and campaign-level initiatives in a hands-on fashion.

Competitive Strategy Workshops: For clients who define themselves not as "second tier players" or "followers" but as "Giant Killers" and who relate to the expression "We're number two . . . and we hate it," we offer a workshop based on agency principal Stephen Denny's book, *Killing Giants: 10 Strategies to Topple the Goliath in Your Industry*. Drawing from over thirty-three case studies from thirteen countries, we present viable solutions to difficult competitive scenarios.

Strategic Marketing Consulting: As a natural follow-on to the outcomes from cosponsoring the Culture & Technology Intersection study and its subsequent work/activation workshop, the principals of Denny Leinberger Strategy will often stay engaged in a second phase to ensure big ideas are carried through to the pilot phase.

Visit us at *DLStrategy.com*.